WHAM!
Teaching with Graphic Novels Across the Curriculum

WILLIAM G. BROZO
GARY MOORMAN
CARLA K. MEYER

Foreword by Stergios Botzakis

TEACHERS COLLEGE PRESS

Teachers College, Columbia University
New York and London

The chapter opening images for Chapters 2 and 4 are reprinted by permission of Hill and Wang, a division of Farrar, Straus and Giroux, LLC: Excerpt from *Trinity: A Graphic History of the First Atomic Bomb* by Jonathan Fetter-Vorm. Copyright © 2012 by Jonathan Fetter-Vorm and Michael Gallagher. Excerpt from *The Stuff of Life: A Graphic Guide to Genetics and DNA* by Mark Schultz, illustrations by Zander Cannon and Kevin Cannon. Text copyright © 2009 by Mark Schultz. Illustrations copyright © 2009 by Zander Cannon and Kevin Cannon.

The chapter opening image for Chapter 3 is reprinted by permission of Classical Comics, © Classical Comics Ltd.

The chapter opening image for Chapter 5 is reprinted by permission of No Starch Press.

The chapter opening image for Chapter 6 is taken from Lesmoir-Gordon, N., Rood, W., & Edney, R. (2009). *Introducing Fractals: A Graphic Guide*. London: Icon Books, and is reprinted by permission of Icon Books Ltd.

Figures 1.1 and 1.4 are reprinted by permission of author Gene Yang.

Published by Teachers College Press, 1234 Amsterdam Avenue, New York, NY 10027

Library of Congress Cataloging-in-Publication Data

Brozo, William G.
    Wham! : teaching with graphic novels across the curriculum / William G. Brozo, Gary Moorman, Carla K. Meyer.
        pages cm. − (Language and literacy series)
    Includes bibliographical references and index.
    ISBN 978-0-8077-5495-5 (pbk. : alk. paper)
    ISBN 978-0-8077-7248-5 (e-book)
    1. Graphic novels in education. 2. Graphic novels—Study and teaching. I. Moorman, Gary B. II. Meyer, Carla K. III. Title.
    LB1044.9.C59B76   2014
    741.5071—dc23   2013029310

ISBN 978-0-8077-5495-5 (paper)
eISBN 978-0-8077-7248-5

Printed on acid-free paper
Manufactured in the United States of America

21 20 19 18 17 16 15 14   8 7 6 5 4 3 2 1

Contents

Foreword

I FREQUENTLY REFER TO GRAPHIC NOVELS in my teacher education classes. Recently, when I distributed various examples for my students to peruse in class, one of them had a moment of enlightenment: "Oh, these are what you were talking about when you said *graphic novels*. These are like comic books. I was wondering why you kept telling us we should include novels full of gratuitous sex and violence when we teach."

This exchange made us all laugh at the time, but it also uncovered two of the biggest barriers to using graphic novels in class. First, the name of the medium is somewhat misleading and causes misconceptions. Most of them are not *graphic* in the lurid sense, and many are not novelistic at all; some are nonfiction and others collections of assorted tales. Second, they use the same sequential art conventions of comic books, which means that they are often equated with those texts and their most popular genre in the United States, superhero adventures. Consequently, they are also easily considered slight texts unworthy of serious consideration. I can explain why in a brief delineation of comic book history.

American comic books were invented in the mid-1930s, and the period from their inception up to about 1950 is commonly called the Golden Age of Comic Books, a period when many popular characters and genres were created. This period ended with a series of hearings in which comic books were associated with rises in juvenile delinquency, followed by the creation of the Comics Code Authority, which ordered that comic book content be suitable for young readers. This code cemented the notion that comic books were solely for children, even though they enjoyed a sizable adult readership—a notion that has continued until the present day and crept into conceptions about graphic novels.

The association of comic books with ill effects did not only exist in the public consciousness, but also existed in the few (less than a handful) educational research studies that focused on these marginalized texts. The results of these studies declared that reading comic books could cripple readers, distracting them with pictures from the print text necessary to build reading stamina or alternatively causing a certain type of dyslexia. These studies began with an assumption that comic books were deleterious. Also, they did not recognize that comic book readers simultaneously had to make sense of two different symbol systems, words and images, in the process of comprehending sequential art, or that, in the words of Alan Purves (1998), comics were multimodal, "an early form of hypertext" (p. 47).

Thus, comic books came to be regarded as disposable and inferior reading matter suitable only for the dim and the childish. They were considered not at all literary, a notion that is problematic and almost definitely false. My own research into adults who read comic books (Botzakis, 2009) found that 92% of participants were actually quite capable readers who read for many of the same reasons associated with literary reading. They just preferred to have pictures combined with their words. So I take umbrage when a broad and false notion about comic books is also applied to graphic novels, especially at the present time, which I consider a sort of Golden Age of Graphic Novels.

The range and complexity of graphic novels being published right now is simply amazing to me. There are books for all ages, on all manner of topics, that apply to any number of content areas—all characteristics that are clearly and repeatedly highlighted in this volume. Graphic novels are not simply books for struggling readers, nor are they stopgaps for more serious reading. They are part of what should be a balanced array of texts that all can read, enjoy, and learn from.

In this volume, William G. Brozo, Gary Moorman, and Carla K. Meyer point to this proliferation, as well as the educative potential, of graphic novels. After reading its pages, I feel others will agree with me that they have done an excellent job pointing out how graphic novel creators such as Jim Ottaviani and Larry Gonick communicate much about history, science, and mathematics while also making connections to comprehension and thinking skills that accompany both literacy and content-specific learning. I feel this book effectively breaks down the two major barriers to using graphic novels—pointing out how they can indeed be substantive, substantial, and meaningful as texts and teaching tools. It is the book I wish my student had read before he came to my class.

—Stergios Botzakis

Preface

THIS BOOK IS AN EXPLORATION of the crossroads of graphic novels and content area instruction. We have been amazed by what a positive writing experience this has been. As university professors, we have done a substantial amount of professional writing, and frankly, it is not always much fun. We believe several factors contributed to our exceptional experience writing this book. First, we had the opportunity to carefully read a variety of graphic novels, which opened our eyes to the expansive body of high-quality selections in this genre. Second, we enjoyed the challenge of creatively thinking about how to integrate graphic novels into the curricula of the different disciplines. Finally, we benefited from working collaboratively with some highly knowledgeable and genial peers.

We decided to write this book because each of us has an interest in content literacy and adolescent learners. We feel that too often content instruction resorts to the banking model of instruction, in which the students are viewed as empty accounts waiting to be filled by the teacher (Freire, 1970). Instead, we advocate instruction that engages students to actively learn and independently acquire knowledge. We believe that graphic novels are an excellent medium to motivate today's youth to become independent learners and thinkers.

ABOUT THIS BOOK

In this book, we provide essential information to help content area teachers think about and develop instruction that integrates graphic novels. In the first chapter, we make the case that graphic novels are a form of youth media whose time has come as a teaching and learning tool in secondary content classrooms. We share valuable information about the history of graphic novels, the unique qualities of today's youth, and the distinct literacies needed to read graphic novels. Chapter 2 provides general guidelines about how to use graphic novels in the content classroom. We recommend methods to review curriculum and identify appropriate inclusion of graphic novels, as well as share advice on how to select high-quality graphic novels for the classroom. In Chapters 3–6, we describe numerous examples of how graphic novels can be successfully integrated into English/language arts, history, science, and mathematics classrooms. In Chapter 7, we provide our perspectives and suggestions about to how to begin the process of incorporating graphic novels into your instruction. The book also includes three appendixes that provide additional information to help you along your journey: Appendix A is a list of graphic novels organized by content area; Appendix B is a collection of professional resources to further your study of graphic novels; and Appendix C addresses how graphic novel instruction aligns with the Common Core State Standards.

ACKNOWLEDGMENTS

No book is written in isolation. We would like to acknowledge the many people who helped us. We would like to thank Margaret Gregor, the Instructional Materials Center Librarian at Appalachian State University, for her tireless support and incredible recommendations. We would also like to thank Melissa Mayville and Archie Hill, doctoral students at George Mason University, as well as Alyssa Miller, Allison Razzeto, Michelle Rhyne, and Jenny McKinnon, graduate students at Appalachian State University, for the invaluable footwork they provided. We would be remiss if we did not mention all the input and wisdom we gained from the practicing teachers who shared their expertise and experience with us. Finally, we would like to thank our editor, Emily Spangler, for her commitment to this project and her thoughtful suggestions at every stage in the book's development.

It is our hope that reading this book will encourage you to explore the world of graphic novels. We believe that such professional journeys are better undertaken with fellow teachers, so we urge you to read this book with your colleagues. We hope you can find the same joy in reading graphic novels that we have found, and take this opportunity to creatively use your newfound knowledge to better your instruction. We believe that your professional life will be richer for the effort and that your students will be the beneficiaries.

CHAPTER ONE

Graphic Novels: Youth Media for the Content Classroom

ANTICIPATION GUIDE				
Directions: Read each statement carefully and decide whether you agree or disagree with it, placing a check mark in the appropriate Before Reading column. When you have finished reading and studying Chapter 1, return to the guide and decide whether your anticipations need to be changed by placing a check mark in the appropriate After Reading column.				
	BEFORE READING		**AFTER READING**	
	Agree	*Disagree*	*Agree*	*Disagree*
1. Graphic novels are another name for comic books.				
2. Graphic novels can build schema for disciplinary content.				
3. Graphic novels are commonplace in most content classrooms.				
4. Graphic novels should be used in disciplinary instruction because of youths' high interest in this medium.				
5. Graphic novels can be used to improve reading skills and critical literacy abilities.				

> Integrating graphic novels into my curriculum has been one of the best choices I have made as a teacher of both high- and lower-level students.
>
> —Lisa Cohen, *But This Book Has Pictures! The Case for Graphic Novels in the AP Classroom*

CONSIDER THE FOLLOWING two teaching scenarios. Both are examples of excellent teaching. Both teachers are considered experts and are highly regarded by their colleagues and supervisors. Their teaching reflects current best practices and their instructional strategies are data based. Students in their classes master course content, achieve goals related to the course, and perform well on end-of-course testing.

Scene One: Traditional High School History Classroom

Experienced history teacher Ms. Jones begins the lesson on the pre–Civil Rights era in the United States by showing an overhead of a graphic organizer that provides students with a visual representation of key vocabulary and concepts. After a brief explanation, she moves to a discussion of a study guide that students completed when they read the chapter assigned for homework the previous night. Most, but not all, students have completed the study guide. Ms. Jones then delivers a lecture that includes the use of overheads, the blackboard, and references to the graphic organizer. Students have the textbook on their desks and take notes using pen and paper. At the conclusion of the lecture, the class is engaged in a discussion. The discussion follows a recitation format, where Ms. Jones poses a question, a student volunteers an answer, and Ms. Jones provides feedback and then asks the next question. A limited number of students volunteer to answer questions; however, most students try to pay attention, as Ms. Jones has stressed that a test on the chapter will be given the next day. As class ends, students are encouraged to review their notes and reread the assigned textbook chapters to prepare for the test.

Scene Two: 21st-Century High School History Classroom

During that same class period, just down the hall, students in another American history class are having very different experiences with a newly minted teacher, Mr. Brown. Younger and active in participatory popular cultural media, Mr. Brown incorporates a variety of texts and media into his lessons, including graphic novels.

During their study of the pre–Civil Rights period, students learn from the textbook broad facts and statistics on Jim Crow, racial segregation, and lynchings of African Americans, especially in the Deep South. Mr. Brown also introduces the class to *Incognegro* (Johnson & Pleece, 2009). This graphic novel gives a name and face to a Black man facing a lynch mob banging at the jailhouse door after he is wrongfully accused of murdering a White woman in Mississippi. Mr. Brown's inclusion of graphic novels in history has produced greater enthusiasm for learning and careful, elaborated processing of textual information. Mr. Brown employs other activities related to graphic novels, including having his students rework important scenes of history into their own illustrated panels, with present-day talk and slang. For students without skill in drawing, Mr. Brown shows how to use sites such as DAZ 3D, Animotions, and Renderosity and download the models, figures, props, and costumes they need for their digital graphic novels. In this way, students do not need artistic abilities to draw, ink, and color their own book panels.

Although these two classrooms have common goals, Mr. Brown is fluent in the language of newer technologies and media. His 21st-century literacy-oriented teaching heightens engagement and learning for his students by (1) eliminating barriers between their outside-of-school interests and literacies and his classroom practices and (2) allowing students to combine the technology and media they increasingly use in their everyday lives with textbook content.

Since this is a book about graphic novels, you are no doubt aware of our preference for the type of teaching presented in the second scenario. This is not to say that we don't recognize the power of the more traditional form of teaching, and in fact we have long advocated the kind of teaching described in the first scenario. We also acknowledge that, at least for the present, there is no research base that unequivocally demonstrates that using digital media, graphic novels, and other print sources will result in greater achievement. We do, however, strongly believe that the 21st-century classroom offers two clear advantages over the more traditional classroom. First, from our viewpoint, one of the overarching goals of education is to help students become highly skilled, enthusiastic, lifelong learners. We live in a fast-paced, highly technical, rapidly changing, global environment. Success demands independent learning and social skills more than knowledge of facts. Second, it is our experience that using graphic novels makes the teaching experience richer and more satisfying. Reading graphic novels is just plain fun, and that's equally as true for teachers as it is for students.

WHY GRAPHIC NOVELS?

In the first peer-reviewed professional article published in a graphic novel format, Yang (2008) begins with the panels shown in Figure 1.1. In the article, Yang illustrates the power of graphic novels, a power derived from their visual nature.

Figure 1.1. Gene Yang's Introduction to Graphic Novels

Human beings are naturally visual learners. Prior to the first writing systems, which appeared about 5,000 years ago, our ancestors relied on visual learning for survival. Jump forward a few millennia, and today's youth have grown up in a highly visual, highly technological environment. They are comfortable with and adept at visual learning. Graphic novels provide today's youth with the opportunity to learn in a medium with which they are comfortable.

For our purposes, we subscribe to Gorman's (2003) hybrid definition of a graphic novel, as "an original book-length story, either fiction or nonfiction, published in comic book style" (p. xii). Carter (2009) suggests that, far from being a new phenomenon, graphic novels as sequential art narratives are as old as ancient cave paintings. Comic books, the precursors to graphic novels, emerged from comic strips that began appearing in newspapers late in the 19th century. The first comic books appeared in the 1920s, and the first superhero comic introduced American youth to Superman in 1938. The 1930s is also when studies of comics in education and sociology journals began to appear (Inge, 1990; Krashen, 2004; Wright, 2001).

Will Eisner's *A Contract with God and Other Tenement Stories*, a series of four stories about his life growing up in the tenements of Brooklyn in the 1930s, was the first book to be labeled a graphic novel when it debuted in 1978. In 1987, *'Nam*, a graphic novel by Doug Murray, won the Best Media of the Vietnam War Award, given by the Bravo Organization, a veterans group. Perhaps the most widely known graphic novel is Art Spiegelman's *Maus: A Survivor's Tale* (1986). In comic book format, this novel presents the horrors of the Holocaust. Immediately, Spiegelman draws readers into this gripping narrative by anthropomorphizing cats as Nazis, mice as Jews, pigs as Poles, and frogs as French. Upon its original release in 1985, *Maus* was acclaimed as a "quiet triumph . . . impossible to achieve in any medium but comics" (Scholz, 1985, p. BW18). Speigelman was awarded a Pulitzer Prize in 1992 for *Maus*. This honor went a long way toward legitimizing and validating graphic novels as a serious literary form, and other serious graphic novelists soon followed (McTaggert, 2005).

Because graphic novels are illustrated and formatted like comic books, confusion persists over the difference between the two. Indeed, the term *comic book* is problematic when used together with *graphic novel* because of the associations with comic strips such as *Peanuts* or *Doonesbury* and light fare from childhood, such as *Archie*. Some helpful distinctions are that graphic novels are usually lengthier and have more complex story lines that make them attractive to mature audiences (Botzakis, 2011). This length, typically between 50 and 175 pages, makes it possible for creators to explore topics and themes in intricate narratives—not possible with the much shorter comic book versions (Gravett, 2005). Graphic novelists are more likely to take on issues and concerns similar to those found in traditional literature. Graphic novels are stand-alone stories, unlike comics, which are often serialized in consecutive parts. And because graphic novels are a dynamic blend of image and word, with illustrations that enrich and extend the text, readers are not only required to decode the words and images but also to identify events occurring between the visual sequences (Simmons, 2003).

The popularity of graphic novels with youth is undeniable. It's the fastest-growing type of young adult literature, with overall sales in the United States and Canada approaching $400 million in 2009 (Reid & Macdonald, 2010). The enthusiasm for graphic novels among youth and adults, as well as their financial success for publishers, are helping to dispel "an aura of seediness and/or violence" (Mackey & McClay, 2000, p. 191). Because the perceptions regarding graphic novels are changing, their numbers continue to grow in public and school libraries (Hajdu, 2004). Educators have now begun to explore the role graphic novels can play in secondary classrooms. This includes enticing adolescent readers into the pages of more canonical texts (Cromer & Clark, 2007) and, as we contend in this book, incorporating them as central texts in content area classrooms.

The research evidence to support the efficacy of using graphic novels to teach history, science, math, and literature still has much room for growth (Gavigan, 2010; Thompson, 2008). We argue that this is due to what Cromer and Clark (2007) characterize as the "very recent journey of this genre towards cultural legitimacy" (p. 575). It is clear that this genre has rich potential for teaching, and the time has come to begin exploring how graphic novels fit into content area instruction.

TRANSITIONING FROM TRADITIONAL TO 21ST-CENTURY TEACHING

The traditional approach to teaching we refer to is based on a narrow view of instruction in which content covered on end-of-course assessments serves as the de facto curriculum (Sipe, 2009). With this emphasis on covering the content, teachers often resort to mentioning rather than teaching (Alexander, 2007). In other words, teachers feel pressure to superficially address content with students so they can cover the content prior to the state-level assessment (Darling-Hammond, 1997). Many teachers feel constrained by this narrow view of instruction (Musoleno & White, 2010). We believe that an in-depth and inclusive approach to teaching better serves today's student. There are several key ingredients that can lead to a shift in the educational environment toward a more relevant approach to teaching and learning. In this section, we will provide very brief descriptions of three elements we consider foundational: theoretical perspectives, the goals of education, and the role of teachers in 21st-century schools.

Theoretical Perspectives

We strongly believe that research-based theory should guide instruction. The field of literacy boasts nearly a century of solid thinking spanning learning to read and write and learning from reading and writing. We have identified two theoretical perspectives as powerful frames of instruction for today's students: schema theory and sociocultural theory.

A schema is a metaphorical place in the mind where knowledge is stored (Anderson & Pearson, 1984; Rumelhart, 1978). Every individual develops schemas based on personal experiences. When new information is encountered, no matter in what form, it is assimilated into existing, related schema. For example, when children first encounter a dog, they create a "dog schema." Each new encounter with a dog enriches the existing schema. Other schemas, for example cats or pets, are related through experience. A good way to look at schemas is that they form a complex filing system. Understanding new information or learning new knowledge is the process of relating the new to the known. From this perspective, teaching is the process of building a bridge between the content to be learned and students' existing schemas or knowledge structures. Learning is accommodating, that is, adjusting, both the new information in relation to what is already known and what is already known to the new information. From our viewpoint, too much of current curriculum efforts, including the Common Core State Standards, focuses only on new content. Graphic novels can help teachers refocus attention on the often rich, but also often impoverished, knowledge structures that students bring with them to school.

A foundational assumption of sociocultural theory is that all learning is social and culturally based. The Russian psychologist Lev Vygotsky (1962, 1978) pointed out that as children learn to speak their native language they begin to use language not just to communicate but to think. Early, in most children by age 3 or 4, language and thought become irreversibly intertwined. All complex ideas appear twice, first socially through oral or written language, then personally, through internalized language. Our personal thoughts amount to an internal, nearly nonstop dialogue with our self. Learning is the process of putting ideas into language, first in social settings (in school, for example), then individually as language is used to further process ideas. Teaching, then, is the process of engaging students in dialogue rich in the language of each discipline, then assisting them in creating unique ideas through their own speech and writing. It is particularly important that students be given ample opportunity to express their thinking through both oral and written language.

Taken together, schema theory and sociocultural theory provide teachers with a number of important principles of instruction. First, it is critical to find out what students already know about the topics being taught. Closely related to this is the interest factor: Students are more familiar with things they are interested in. Providing instruction that is relevant and related to students' lives outside of school is the cornerstone of good teaching. Finally, teachers must realize that language is the first tool of learning. Since humans use language to think with, it is crucial that students be given rich opportunities as well as instruction in both receptive language (listening and reading) and expressive language (speaking and writing).

The Goals of Education

One ingredient lacking in current educational debates is a serious exploration of the broad overall goals of education. The goal of the No Child Left Behind Act (NCLB) was to have all children reading and performing in mathematics at grade level. This goal was based on a false understanding of the concept of grade level (which is the average score of all children at a particular grade) as well as of the reality of wide variance of performance on any learning activity. In reality, not all children can be above average. The stated goal of the current Common Core State Standards (CCSS) initiative is to make all students career- and/or college-ready upon graduation. While this is a laudable and more reasonable goal to guide our educational system, it still, in our opinion, falls below the higher-order goals necessary for modern schooling.

In America, our school system was founded on the premise that education is crucial for a democratic form of government. The Founding Fathers recognized that majority rule by an uneducated population would end in mob rule. History has proved them correct; successful democracies have highly functioning school systems, and attempts to impose democracies on countries with low educational levels are uniformly unsuccessful. Therefore, a primary goal of education must be to assist students in becoming responsible citizens in a democratic society, and increasingly in an emerging global community as well.

The idea of global citizenship is tied to the reality of a rapidly changing economic and political reality. We live in an era where change is the only constant. Many of today's best jobs did not exist 10 years ago. Technology and research open new doors of understanding every day. For example, in medicine, surgeries that used to require invasive procedures and extended hospital stays are now routinely done arthroscopically on an outpatient basis. The economic opportunities that new knowledge and technology provide are open only to those who are lifelong, enthusiastic learners and readers.

In summary, two overarching goals provide the navigation for the thinking that guided the writing of this book. First, that schooling must prepare students to be active, well-informed citizens of a democratic society and global community. And second, that schooling must assist students in becoming lifelong, enthusiastic learners and readers.

The Role of Teachers in 21st-Century Schools

It is crucial, from our perspective, to view teachers as professionals and teaching as a complex activity that requires ongoing, in-context decision-making. One of the most damaging trends in current educational policy is what many refer to as the deskilling of teachers (e.g., Baumann, 1992; Kraft, 1995). This refers to tying teachers to predetermined curriculum and scripted lessons. In contrast, we believe that the best teaching occurs when teachers operate within accepted guidelines but with the freedom to adapt in-class instruction based on the needs and background of their students. The kind of creative teaching we advocate in this book is impossible if teachers are hand-cuffed by local, state, or federal mandates that limit their decision-making.

In this section we have developed a theoretical framework justifying the integration of graphic novels into disciplinary classrooms. Obviously, this will require major changes in the way most teachers manage their classrooms and implement instruction. We recognize that the current political context in education as well as traditional approaches to teaching will make the changes we recommend in this book difficult. We do not encourage a dramatic, overnight change. Teachers need to be thoughtful and deliberate when making substantive changes. We encourage you to think in terms of evolution, not revolution.

THE COMMON CORE STATE STANDARDS AND GRAPHIC NOVELS

We sense and hope for a change in the educational environment. We believe that the CCSS invite the integration of graphics novels into the curriculum. The CCSS increase the expectation for students to not only acquire information but to utilize a variety of thinking skills to analyze the information as well (Rothman, 2012). The CCSS provide literacy standards for English/language arts as well as literacy standards for the history/social studies, sciences, and technical subjects and were designed to help students attain the skills and knowledge needed for college and career readiness in the 21st century (National Governors Association Center for Best Practices, Council of Chief State School Officers, 2010). We believe the time is ripe for content teachers to embrace instruction that will help all students engage in learning through a variety of texts, including graphic novels. The following are a few examples of how the integration of graphic novels and the literacies required to read graphic novels align with the Common Core. These standards focus on students in grades 6–12 and include standards from both English language arts as well as standards for literacy in history/social studies, science, and the technical subjects. We believe that graphic novels integrated into thoughtful, well-planned lessons can address any of the CCSS Anchor Standards for Reading. However, the use of graphic novels explicitly addresses the following anchor standards:

Integration of Knowledge and Ideas

Standard 7: Integrate and evaluate content presented in diverse formats and media, including visually and quantitatively, as well as words.
Standard 9: Analyze how two or more texts address similar themes and topics in order to build knowledge or compare the approaches the authors take.

Range of Reading and Level of Text Complexity

Standard 10: Read and comprehend complex literary and information texts independently and proficiently.

Incorporating graphic novels into the content classroom provides an engaging platform for teachers to address the demands of the CCSS. To further investigate this, let's look at Standard 7. Graphic novels tell a story through prose, dialogue, and visual images, so graphic novels are a natural fit to help students learn to comprehend, evaluate, and integrate information ascertained through media other than traditional print. We also believe that graphic novels used in tandem with traditional forms of text will foster students' ability to analyze multiple texts as required in Standard 9. Finally, high-quality graphic novels have evolved into extremely complex works of literature that fulfill the CCSS guidelines for text complexity. For example, *Trinity: A Graphic History of the First Atomic Bomb* (Fetter-Vorm, 2013) addresses both the quantitative and qualitative complexity demands of the CCSS. Careful planning and integration of graphic novels will ensure that the reading and task demands are met as well.

GRAPHIC NOVELS, MULTIPLE LITERACIES, AND TODAY'S YOUTH

In this section, we ask disciplinary teachers to take a new look at the possibilities for teaching using a variety of texts, specifically graphic novels. There are two compelling factors behind this request. First, today's students are the products of a social environment radically different from that of any time in history. Today's students have grown up with computers, cell phones, and other digital technology. Prensky (2005–2006) refers to them as digital natives, fluent in the language, skills, and attitudes of a high-tech environment. We would argue they are the best-read and the most well-informed generation ever. Consider these characteristics of 16- to 29-year-olds taken from a study done by the Pew Internet and American Life Project (Zickuhr, Rainie, Purcell, Madden, & Brenner, 2012):

- 83% read at least one book in the last year.
- 95% have cell phones; 80% have a desktop or laptop.
- 96% use the Internet.
- Mean number of books read in the last year is: 17.
- Americans under age 30 are more likely than older adults to do reading of any sort.

Any systematic analysis of today's adolescents leads to the conclusion that they bring to school a different and highly sophisticated set of learning skills and attitudes. We have every reason to believe that students will become even more well-informed, literate, and technologically sophisticated learners in future generations.

The second compelling factor is the increasing demand that the 21st century is making and will continue to make in terms of literacy skill and expertise. Consider that in 1940, less than half the U.S. population had completed 8th grade and only 6% of males and 4% of females had completed college (National Center for Education Statistics, 1993). Thirty years ago cell phones came in briefcases and the Internet was accessible only to individuals who could write computer code. Obviously, times have changed dramatically, along with the knowledge and skills necessary for success. Current expectations are that students will leave school with high levels of reading skill. But more importantly, it is clear that literacy entails more than just reading and writing. Success as adults certainly will require high-level literacy skills with print media. But it will also require visual and technical literacy. Outside of school, students live in a complex social and economic environment centered on computers, the Internet, and other digital technologies. So in many ways today's youth are up to the ever-increasing demands they face. Their use of digital technology to access information, engage socially, and solve problems is impressive. The world of knowledge is at their fingertips.

Today in most traditional upper-grades classrooms there remain two ever-present, authoritative information sources—the teacher and the textbook (Walker & Bean, 2002). Yet youth of the digital age have access to and facility with a wide array of richly informative print and multimedia sources. Furthermore, it has been asserted that providing content in a variety of forms of representation increases students' abilities to think and communicate using different symbol systems (Collier, 2007; Grisham & Wolsey, 2006; Schwarz, 2002) and develops critical visual literacy (Cromer & Clark, 2007).

We know from our own experiences and those of our innovative middle and high school colleagues that when graphic novels and other alternative texts and information sources are given legitimacy in content classrooms, youth are more eager to explore disciplinary topics and learning is more memorable. These sources, while going largely untapped in traditional school settings, may hold the key to engaging adolescents in meaningful reading and learning as well as elevating their achievement. Thus, we do not advocate suppression of textbooks but the inclusion of graphic novels to enrich teaching and learning in the content classroom. Graphic novels accompanied by a variety of supportive technology tools have the potential to transform bland, textbook-centered learning environments into exciting venues for authentic exploration of disciplinary topics.

According to Kist (as cited by Collier, 2007), "Out-of-school (and workplace) literacies are becoming more divergent from in-school literacies" (p. 5). Yet skillful use of the sources and practices of youth literacies may be the way to capture students' interest in traditional school topics (Chun, 2009). Teaching with graphic novels, an alternative to traditional instruction, can develop and draw on students' multiliterate practices. Moreover, with our increasingly complex global information and communication systems, students can only benefit from exposure to and grounding in multiple modes of representation. A multimodal text like a graphic novel would seem to be ideally suited to this purpose.

Only within the past 2 decades have researchers begun to focus on the variety of ways youth learn literacies, the interconnecting contexts in which literacies are learned, and young adults' multiple purposes for engaging in literate practices. This scholarship has emphasized the role of multimodal forms of representation and meaning-making in the lives of young people (Cope & Kalantzis, 2000; Vasudevan & Campano, 2009). Multiliteracies are defined as "the multiplicity of communication channels and media" (Cope & Kalantzis, 2000, p. 5). Those on the vanguard of multiliteracies (New London Group, 1996) argue that "literacy pedagogy must now account for the burgeoning variety of text forms associated with information and multimedia technologies" (p. 60). Many (Alvermann, 2002; Dredger, Woods, Beach, & Sagstetter, 2010; Goodman, 2003; Kajder, 2010; Kress & Van Leeuwen, 2001; Zenkov, Bell, Harmon, Ewaida, & Fell, 2011) urge schools to make room in language and disciplinary curricula for students' different experiences that are expressed through a variety of media. Graphic novels with their multimodalities and their engaging content can be used to encourage students to build knowledge, read more deeply, and think more critically about both print and image.

Calls for secondary schools to honor the literacies and discourses of youth derive from the realization that we live in a mediasphere (O'Brien, 2001), "a world saturated by inescapable, ever-evolving, and competing media that both flow through us and are altered and created by us" (Brozo, 2005, p. 534). Adolescents are the most active participants in the mediasphere, creating forms of discourse that should be integrated into school settings, since competency in these new forms of communication will benefit them later in life (Lankshear & Knobel, 2002; Vasudevan & Campano, 2009). The discourse worlds that most teens inhabit offer them a kind of "language of intimacy" (Dowdy, 2002, p. 4) that if validated in schools and classrooms could increase engagement in literacy and learning. Secondary classrooms are the setting where youths' multiple literacies—digital, graphic, and aural—can lead to understanding, critical analysis, and reinterpretation of concepts and content.

Another reason to create room in the curriculum for out-of-school competencies with new literacies and media relates to developing academic knowledge and skills. For example, Chun (2009) used multiliteracies pedagogy with Spiegelman's *Maus* in a class of English language learners (ELLs). He found that the graphic novel nurtured students' critical awareness of their world. Using the ELL students as a resource, Chun explored the graphic novel's power to teach them to make meaningful connections to their own lives and reflect critically on how the themes of racism and power in *Maus* operate in their own worlds. Chun summarizes his work by asserting:

> Using a graphic novel like *Maus* in the classroom to teach how language works both for and against people can enable students to acquire the necessary critical literacy that will, as Freire and Macedo (1987) affirmed, aid them in the important tasks of reading both the world and the word. (p. 152)

It's clear that those responsible for providing adolescent and content literacy instruction need to know more about the funds of knowledge, discourse competencies, and textual practices that youth bring with them to middle and secondary school classrooms (Jetton & Dole, 2004; Strickland & Alvermann, 2004). Coming to know students in this way will lead to more responsive instruction that integrates in- and beyond-school literacy and learning experiences (Lee, 1997; Moje et al., 2004; Schultz, 2002).

THE LITERACY DEMANDS OF
GRAPHIC NOVELS AND COMICS

With the popularity of graphic novels among today's youth, it is safe to say that many secondary students already have experience reading them. Some of them may be expert graphic novel readers, and teachers should turn to these experts to help identify and integrate good graphic novels into their classrooms. However, teachers cannot assume that all students are graphic novel experts. We believe that in order for teachers to successfully integrate graphic novels into their instruction, they must first learn to be expert readers of the format themselves.

Reading Graphic Novels

Novels, picture books, film, and poetry all tell us a story in their own unique ways. Novels tell a story in linear narrative, picture books through text supported by illustrations, film through moving images and dialogue, and poetry through written imagery. Graphic novels are a distinct form of storytelling that combines elements from all these media. Unlike these media, graphic novels use all these techniques to tell a story (Scholastic, 2013). The reader must simultaneously process both print and artwork to follow the narrative. Navigating this format requires a different set of literacy skills.

As professors, we often ask our graduate students, who are usually practicing teachers, to read graphic novels. For some of them, it is the first time they have read a graphic novel. We usually teach an introductory lesson in which prior to any instruction, we ask our students to read from a self-selected graphic novel for about 15 minutes. For the students who have never read a graphic novel, this activity proves to be quite challenging. We often hear phrases such as "I read too fast to get any meaning," and "I didn't pay close enough attention to the illustrations." These graphic novel novices do not recognize that the format requires the reader to approach the text and illustrations in tandem. The words and pictures in graphic novels must be carefully analyzed because the authors/illustrators of high-quality graphic novels make purposeful choices in relation to the words, speech bubbles, pictures, format, color, and other graphic features in their book.

Expert readers of traditional text focus on print in order to comprehend a story. When reading graphic novels, it is necessary to slow down and give attention to the many different elements of a story. In addition to the printed text, visual images, color, font style and size, visual perspectives, and other graphic elements convey important information. The reader must also identify focal points of the visual images and determine the directionality of the frames. Being able to make inferences is also crucial in understanding a graphic novel. When learning to effectively navigate graphic novels, readers must develop a set of skills that allows them to process all elements of the medium to make sense of authors' stories. As teachers, learning these skills will help you to better incorporate graphic novels into your classroom instruction.

The Language of Graphic Novels

To read, discuss, and write in a specific content, the learner must have command of the language associated with the content (Jetton & Alexander, 2004). The same holds true for reading, writing, and discussing a specific genre or format of literature. In order to successfully integrate graphic novels into their instruction, teachers must pay particular attention to the language and structure of this format. Entire books have been dedicated to understanding comics and graphic novels (e.g., Eisner, 2008). In particular, McCloud (1994) deeply delves into the language of graphic novels. Since our intent is to help you integrate graphic novels into instruction, we can dedicate only a small portion of space to this topic. If you are interested in learning more, we recommend further reading on this topic.

Using the McCloud (1994) and Eisner (2008) books as well as a website (No Flying No Tights, 2013), we have identified the words shown in Figure 1.2 as key introductory terms for this format. When presenting these key concepts, visuals often help to build a stronger conceptualization for the terms. For

Figure 1.2. Key Graphic Novel Terminology

Key Graphic Novel Vocabulary	Novice-Friendly Explanation
Sequential Art	Images displayed in succession to convey information or a story.
Comics	Cartoons, comic strips, comic books, and graphic novels are all examples of sequential art.
Manga	The Japanese word for comics. In the United States, manga is often associated with anime, a Japanese form of animation.
Manwha	The Korean word for comics. Manwha shares a similar style with manga.
Panel	Picture or image usually laid out within a border. Panels are often an equivalent to a scene from a movie or TV show.
Frame	The border or edge of a panel. While typically a rectangular shape, the author may change the shape to convey meaning to the reader.
Gutter	The white space between frames. The gutter is one of the most important narrative tools in comics.
Bleed	When the art runs off of the page instead of being contained by a border. A bleed is sometimes used to convey space or emphasize action.
Graphic Weight	Describes how certain images draw the reader's eye more than others.
Sound Representation	Sound effects represented without speech bubbles and usually written or drawn in a way that highlights their nature (e.g., BAM!, SPLAT!).
Speech Balloon	A graphic tool used to convey ownership of dialogue by a particular character.
Thought Balloon	A graphic tool used to convey ownership of thought by a particular character.
Caption	A narrative device used to convey information that cannot be presented through art, speech, or thought.

example, the graphic organizer shown in Figure 1.3 represents the semantic relationship between the forms of sequential art. In addition, showing examples of panels with key word examples can help reinforce key terminology associated with this medium, as shown in Figure 1.4.

Figure 1.3. Sequential Art Vocabulary Concept Circle

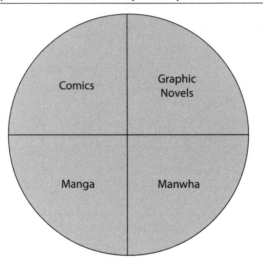

LOOKING BACK AND MOVING FORWARD

In this chapter we argue that graphic novels are a form of youth media whose time has come as a teaching and learning tool in secondary content classrooms. They are a versatile teaching resource that when put in the hands of skillful teachers can heighten student engagement, build knowledge of disciplinary topics, and expand students' literacy capacities. We illustrate how graphic novels relate to the literacy practices of youth outside of school and to the multiliteracies crucial for success in today's social, economic, and political environments. Finally, we discuss the literacy skills required to expertly read graphic novels and comics.

Chapter 2 provides general guidelines for their use in content classrooms. Chapters 3, 4, 5, and 6 are devoted to developing instruction in the disciplines of English/language arts, history, science, and mathematics, respectively. In these chapters, we also suggest additional graphic novels related to the disciplines. In Chapter 7 we provide perspectives and suggestions for moving forward and integrating graphic novels into your instruction. In each chapter we include study questions that can be used to further discuss and explore ideas presented in the

Figure 1.4. Sequential Art Vocabulary Visuals

chapters. Finally, we include three appendices: Appendix A provides extended lists of graphic novels organized by discipline; Appendix B suggests additional resources you can access to further your exploration of graphic novels; and Appendix C illustrates how the instruction we present in Chapters 3 through 6 interfaces with the Common Core State Standards.

Study Group Questions for Chapter 1

- Why would integrating graphic novels into content area instruction benefit today's students?
- What theoretical perspectives guide your instruction?
- How is reading a graphic novel different from reading a traditional novel?
- Imagine you are presenting a rationale for using graphic novels to your school board. What would you include in your argument?

CHAPTER TWO

Guidelines for Using Graphic Novels in the Content Classroom

ANTICIPATION GUIDE

Directions: Read each statement carefully and decide whether you agree or disagree with it, placing a check mark in the appropriate Before Reading column. When you have finished reading and studying Chapter 2, return to the guide and decide whether your anticipations need to be changed by placing a check mark in the appropriate After Reading column.

	BEFORE READING		AFTER READING	
	Agree	*Disagree*	*Agree*	*Disagree*
1. Graphic novels should replace textbooks.				
2. Graphic novels are ideal for unit-based teaching.				
3. Content teachers need to find ways of making time for graphic novels.				
4. Selecting graphic novels for a unit should be based on unit themes.				
5. One graphic novel or multiple graphic novels can be incorporated into disciplinary instruction.				
6. A colleague's recommendation is sufficient for selecting and using a graphic novel in your classroom.				

As these panels make clear, the sophisticated illustrations and rich, informative narration mark *The Stuff of Life: A Graphic Guide to Genetics and DNA* (Schultz, Cannon, & Cannon, 2009) as a distinctively useful resource for teaching science.

Since comics are seen as outside of the imposed discourses of educational institutions, students feel a greater ownership of comics texts, and thus a greater investment in reading them.

—Damian Duffy, *Out of the Margins . . . into the Panels: Toward a Theory of Comics as a Medium of Critical Pedagogy in Library Instruction*

THE CONTRIBUTIONS THAT GRAPHIC NOVELS can make to the teaching of disciplinary content are limited only by one's imagination and willingness to explore the instructional possibilities of this powerful medium. For some, content lessons with graphic novels may be as simple as making this resource available to students without formal or explicit connections to the core text and content. For others, the graphic novel will play a central role in content instruction, read and referred to often throughout a lesson or unit. In any case, of overarching importance is that disciplinary teachers strive to take greater advantage of the wide variety of graphic novels available to them and their students.

We realize that in most secondary schools across the United States textbooks have not become passé, even though this print medium of distilled information and ideas is often singled out as a likely culprit in adolescent students' disaffection with reading (Brozo & Simpson, 2007). When compared with television, video and computer games, and the Internet, school textbooks are becoming an even harder sell to today's youth. Furthermore, in the era of Common Core State Standards, traditional school textbooks are no longer considered the ideal source material for teaching students how to read complex prose. This is because textbook publishers, due to demands of limited space, adoption committees, and readability constraints, produce contrived and overly scaffolded prose. Nonetheless, the textbook industry is big business, and when schools and districts lay out large sums of money for adoptions of certain titles, there is an expectation that the books will be an integral part of instruction, regardless of the feelings of students and their teachers.

Our own position on textbooks is that they may continue to serve a purpose in secondary classroom instruction; however, they should not dictate the pacing and coverage of topics and content. As one resource among several, textbooks offer teachers and students a repository of facts and information. This emphasis, though, on important facts, broad views, pivotal characters, and general effects on whole populations inevitably results in a detached tone and dry material.

In this book we do not advocate suppression of textbooks but the inclusion of graphic novels to enrich teaching and learning in the content classroom. We urge the use of graphic novels as a critical supplement to textbooks because we know that youth will quickly turn off to reading if they find texts difficult or boring (Guthrie & Wigfield, 2000; McPhail, Pierson, & Freeman, 2000). On the other hand, texts and media that youth find familiar and interesting, like graphic novels, can be powerful motivators for reading, writing, and learning (Guthrie, 2007; Seyfried, 2008). As we will demonstrate, in addition to helping students become more engaged and thoughtful learners, these unique texts can serve as important schema-builders, providing the foundation for easier assimilation of new content information and ideas.

The duration and scope of any lesson or series of lessons that integrates graphic novels will depend on the topic and on your judgments and preferences. We endorse the guidelines of the Common Core State Standards, which stress the benefits of planning and teaching in units, whereby students experience a se-ries of lessons often lasting up to several days or even weeks that revolve around a unifying text, such as a graphic novel, or theme with related subtopics. The primary benefit of this approach to teachers and students alike is time—sufficient time to investigate a topic thoroughly and engage in deep and rigorous reading, discussion, writing, and research, and therefore time to get interested in and excited about learning while expanding knowledge. The following guidelines and methods for teaching with graphic novels are most applicable to unit-based teaching.

IDENTIFYING SALIENT THEMES FOR DISCIPLINARY UNITS

The process of identifying important themes and concepts for a unit of study is essential for integrating appropriate graphic novels into related lessons. Over-arching themes and concepts related to the most important information and ideas of the unit will serve as a bridge to connect graphic novels, the textbook, and other sources. The process involves, first, deciding what you want your students to know as a result of the unit and then using this theme as a guide, identifying the related concepts and subtopics.

Indications of important themes and concepts may be extracted from text-books, which are usually organized by units. However, even when textbooks have identifiable units, they often lack explicit development of important themes. Therefore, unit themes that are meaningful to students must be inferred, regard-less of the space and treatment given to particular topics in the textbook.

Themes may also be apparent in the content standards from the Common Core or other curriculum guides. Nevertheless, a theme should not be con-fused with a standard. For instance, a social studies standard may state that 8th-graders should know the causes of the American Civil War, whereas a theme or concept for content related to the Civil War would tell students why they are learning the content, as in "War may be necessary to eliminate human slavery," the theme for social studies teacher Debbie. In fact, the best themes are those that help students think across cultural, geographical, and time boundaries so that new understandings have meaning in their own lives and in different learning contexts.

Brown (2001), for instance, paired with great success William Faulkner's *Light in August* with Art Spiegelman's classic and award-winning graphic novel *Maus* in an English class to demonstrate for students how themes of racism and cultural dominion by Whites existed in the pre-Civil Rights era in the southern United States, the setting of Faulkner's book, as it did in Nazi-dominated Europe, through Spiegelman's allegory with pigs, cats, and mice. She also used *Maus* to help students explore the theme of racism in their own lives and worlds.

The following questions may be helpful to ask of standards and textbooks to derive meaningful themes:

- What are the driving human forces that underlie the information and concepts of these standards or this content?
- What phenomena described or implied in the standards or textbook have affected ordinary people (including me and my students) or may do so in the future?
- What universal patterns of behavior related to this topic should be explained?

Answers to these questions should provide direction for selecting appropriate graphic novels to relate to the theme. For example, when Gabriel, a 7th-grade science teacher, asks similar questions about genetics as presented in the science curriculum standards and the textbook, he identifies the following theme for the upcoming unit on the topic: *Genetic diversity and mutation are the keys to life.*

In seeking graphic novels that might be included in the unit, Gabriel reviews those that contain accurate content, are visually rich and explanatory, and employ an engaging narrative. He decides on Schultz, Cannon, and Cannon's *The Stuff of Life: A Graphic Guide to Genetics and DNA* (2009), because it offers an in-depth description of how atoms form the "stuff" that makes up life, such as proteins, chemicals, and genetic materials. There are ample, very detailed black-and-white illustrations in this 150-page graphic novel. The text is closely matched to each illustrated frame. The book does an excellent job explaining complex concepts in a very dense, technical format. The novel begins with the basics of how atoms assemble into the building blocks of life, RNA and DNA, then moves on to describe the process of inheritance, dominant and recessive traits, and genetic mutations. The book briefly describes current efforts of the Human Genome Project in mapping out DNA for our species. The authors also touch on some of the social and political issues that surround genetics, such as cloning. They also take the time to discuss the important contributions made by key scientists in the discovery of the structure of DNA.

What sets this very technical graphic novel apart from others and the textbook, to Gabriel's mind, is the premise on which it is based, an intelligent race of sea-cucumber-like species called Squinch. Their species lacks the genetic diversity needed for a successful reproductive strategy. Bloort 183, the chief scientist, comes to the rescue as he presents a report on Earth's successful DNA and genetic strategy and how genetic diversity is critical to the success of their species. The story line is clever and adds the "hook" to draw in the reader to the very technical text. The technical information is presented at a rapid pace, but it is the Squinch who help to redirect the pace for understanding. Gabriel also knows that his students will be able to take full advantage of the ample black-and-white illustrations to support their understanding of the material covered in the narrative. The glossary is also very complete and includes illustrations. Another nice addition to the novel for Gabriel is the extended recommended reading section.

IDENTIFYING RELATED CONCEPTS AND SUBTOPICS

After establishing a theme for the unit on genetics, Gabriel's next step is to explore the content further to identify important concepts and subtopics related to the unit's theme. This process leads to the identification of other graphic novels and resources that might be used to support learning for his students. To accomplish this, Gabriel creates a visual display or a web (Brozo & Simpson, 2007). Beginning with the unit theme written in the center of a large piece of paper, he generates related subtopics and writes them around the theme. These ideas come directly from the text, the content standards, and Gabriel's prior knowledge. His unit's theme is broad enough to encompass important concepts and subconcepts such as evolution, cloning, RNA, and DNA while also giving his students a direction for their learning. The subtopic of genetic mutations leads Gabriel to discover the graphic novel *Decoding Genes with Max Axiom, Super Scientist* (Keyser, Smith, & Milgrom, 2010).

In this series of graphic novels, Max Axiom, super scientist, dons his lab coat and takes the reader on a scientific adventure. In *Decoding Genes with Max Axiom, Super Scientist,* Max uses his superpowers to travel back in time to meet Gregor Mendel. Mendel is introduced in his famous pea patch, where Max describes heredity, the structure of genes, and genetic mutation. Max shrinks to the size of an atom to enter the plant to explore and unravel the secrets of genetic coding. Bold, colorful illustrations help explain how geneticists contribute to medicine, agriculture, and conservation.

With features of a textbook such as a table of contents, glossary, and index, students are able to practice skills needed to navigate more traditional textbooks. The information is engaging and presented in a clear manner with vivid illustrations. As part of a series, the single-topic book offers struggling or reluctant readers a helpful and engaging resource. Important vocabulary terms are referenced in the index, defined in the vocabulary, and highlighted within the text. Finally, because the story line is limited to the scientific explanation of genes and heredity and the ample text provides information that is both accurate and well presented, this is an ideal text to complement the science textbook.

Gabriel now has two graphic novels he plans on making available to his science students during the unit on genetics. His next major decisions revolve around how the graphic novels, textbook, and other print and nonprint materials might be organized and integrated into the unit. In the next section, we will describe ways in which the disciplinary classroom can be organized to ensure effective instruction of content and literacy with graphic novels as well as the flexible delivery of these valuable resources.

Figure 2.1 is an example of a web constructed by Debbie for her 8th-grade social studies class for their unit on the American Civil War. By graphically depicting the relationships among different aspects of the overall theme, the web reveals the scope of the unit. This approach can help students to tie information together, expand schema, and improve their overall understanding of the topic. Once Debbie finalizes her web, she locates graphic novels that could help support learning of the various topics and subtopics of the unit (see Figure 2.2).

Figure 2.1. Web for the American Civil War

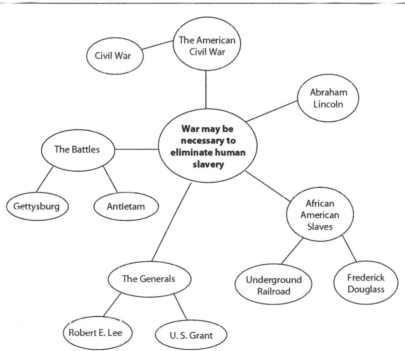

Figure 2.2. Graphic Novels for Civil War Topics and Subtopics

ABRAHAM LINCOLN

Abraham Lincoln: From the Log Cabin to the White House (Campfire, 2012)

Lewis Helfand and Manikandan tell Lincoln's story from his childhood to presidency in rich, informative prose and with vivid illustrations. The authors focus on his most significant presidential and national contribution, the passing of the 13th Amendment, which abolished slavery in the United States.

The Murder of Abraham Lincoln (NBM Publishing, 2005)

Author Rich Geary's meticulous research and vivid illustrations create a fascinating narrative that covers the 62 days between March 4 and May 4, 1865, and provide a wealth of information on murderous thespian and Southern loyalist John Wilkes Booth and his co-conspirators.

SLAVERY

Harriet Tubman and the Underground Railroad (Capstone, 2005)

Michael Martin and Bill Anderson explore Harriet Tubman's heroic life from escaping slavery to establishing the Underground Railroad to help other slaves escape. The graphic novel includes additional facts, a glossary, helpful Internet sites, recommended books, and a bibliography.

Slavery's Storm (Chester Comix, 2003)

Bentley Boyd lays out the political arguments over slavery in the days before the Civil War through the illustrated stories of Nat Turner, Dred Scott, and John Brown.

Cleburne: A Graphic Novel (Rampart Press, 2008)

Justin Murphy wrote and Milgrom and Brown illustrated this remarkable tale of a little-known Confederate general, Patrick Cleburne, who, because of his effort to ensure freedom for all Black soldiers, demonstrated courage in the face of racism, conspiracy, and war.

ORGANIZING THE CONTENT
AND THE CLASSROOM FOR GRAPHIC NOVELS

As we have demonstrated, graphic novels have the potential to significantly influence learning in the disciplines and affect young adults deeply. Even teachers who have positive attitudes about graphic novels as a possible instructional tool but have yet to use them may be hesitant because of uncertainty about (1) how to make time for graphic novels and (2) how to manage a classroom with 20 to 30 students when multiple texts are employed.

It is not unfair to assert that traditional disciplinary curriculum has been overly fragmented and fact laden (Clarke & Agne, 1997; Derry, Schunn, &

Figure 2.2. Graphic Novels for Civil War Topics and Subtopics (continued)

FREDERICK DOUGLASS

The Hammer and the Anvil: Frederick Douglass, Abraham Lincoln, and the End of Slavery in America (Hill and Wang, 2012)

Dwight Zimmerman, along with illustrator Wayne Vansant, highlights the central debates of the Civil War era—race, freedom, citizenship, state versus federal government—through the lives of two giants of the time, Abraham Lincoln and Frederick Douglass, whose parallel lives eventually converged in friendship.

THE GENERALS

Robert E. Lee: The Story of the Great Confederate General (Capstone Press, 2010)

Terry Collins recounts the story of this Southern general from his many victories in several crucial battles, in spite of believing it was a mistake for the South to fight in the Civil War, to his surrender.

THE BATTLES

Gettysburg: The Graphic History of America's Most Famous Battle and the Turning Point of the Civil War (Zenith Press, 2013)

Wayne Vansant describes the events leading up to this pivotal battle as well as the major activity during the 3-day fight between Union and Confederate armies. The portraits of the army leaders, such as Robert E. Lee, James Longstreet, and George Meade, add to this gripping tale of the deadliest battle of the entire war.

The Bloodiest Day: Battle of Antietam (Random House, 2006a)

Larry Hama takes us back to one of the bloodiest days in American history as Union and Confederate armies fought on a stretch of Maryland countryside known as Antietam. From the broad killing field, Hama focuses on the lives of two soldiers who faced each other in a desperate struggle for survival.

Gernsbacher, 2005). This results in students being forced to memorize countless small bits of information in content areas taught as separate and distinct from one another. The amount of time necessary to teach and learn the small details at a rapid pace leaves little room for exploring themes, deeper meanings, and personally relevant applications. As a result, argue Brozo and Simpson (2007), "many students rarely enjoy or see the point in studying history or science facts, forget them, and often have to relearn them the next year. In contrast, time spent exploring various other texts and media can be both efficient and effective because it gets students interested in learning the content and, when the sources are chosen appropriately, can serve as the material for content instruction" (p. 263).

Discipline-related graphic novels are not only engaging to youth but are also rich in content. For example, one of the sources used by Lily, a middle-grades math teacher, for a unit on fractions is *Manga Math Mysteries 5: The Ancient Formula; A Mystery with Fractions* (Theilbar & Pantoja, 2011). This manga-style book serves as an excellent accompanying text for her general math students. In this fifth book of a series, Lily's students are drawn into an engaging story about a group of friends who learn a new math skill and then have the opportunity to apply their newly learned skills. The story is centered on the friends' kung fu activities. The students are anxious to learn to work with the sword, which they are first introduced to by the kung fu master Sifu Faiza. She demonstrates some sword moves and then tells the students that if you only learn three of the moves, you are only learning one-third of the moves because there is a total of nine moves. They anxiously begin practice, but soon tire and take a break to look through Sifu's grandfather's journal. They discover that her grandfather had written down several puzzles. In the journal, Sifu's grandfather had recorded a formula for an ancient medicine, *Jow*. The formula was carved onto an ivory disc divided into eight wedges, but some of the wedges were blank and the original formula had disappeared. The challenge for the kung fu students is to use the clues provided in the journal and their mathematical skills in fractions in order to learn about the ancient formula.

The use of visual representations of fractions makes the concepts, such as denominators and recognizing and comparing fractions, easy to for Lily's students to grasp. The mathematical examples used are well presented and explained to ensure that Lily's students understand them. She chooses this selection also for the colorful and energetic illustrations and the way the authors seamlessly integrate the mathematics of fractions into the story. Because Lily's students learn accurate and applicable information about fractions while enjoying a fun manga-style graphic novel, she is able to use unit time more efficiently than if she relies exclusively on the textbook or some other similar source.

We believe that the best way to approach the problem of finding time to make use of graphic novels is to choose the most important topics and subtopics from the unit web and then place instructional emphasis on them. Naturally, some of the textbook content is not as pertinent to the important themes as other content and, consequently, should be given less attention. Making decisions about which content and concepts to focus on frees up time that can be spent on relevant, important information.

Consider 8th-grade social studies teacher Debbie's unit on the American Civil War. Once her web is completed and graphic novels are identified that could support learning of various topics and subtopics, she then has to prioritize content in order to ensure that emphasis is given to topics related to her unit's theme—in this case, how war may be necessary to end human slavery. With this theme as a guide, Debbie decides to stress the topic of African American Slaves, which includes the subtopics of the Underground Railroad and Frederick Douglass. She also realizes that her students will understand the unit's theme at a deeper and more meaningful level if Abraham Lincoln's presidency, character, and motivations are explored; thus, that topic on her web will also be given a great share of instructional time. It is important to point out that in Debbie's making decisions about what to emphasize in the unit, her students still receive instruction related to all the topics on her web. Content related to the battles and generals, for instance, will be covered in ways that make more time for the most important aspects of the unit.

MANAGING THE CLASSROOM WITH GRAPHIC NOVELS

With respect to the concern about how to manage the content classroom when graphic novels are added, we describe the experiences of three different teachers whose approaches represent three management systems.

Reading Aloud

In explaining why teachers should include graphic novels and comics in read-alouds, Peter Gutierrez says that this approach seems like a leisure activity for students, so they will gain knowledge and skills without realizing it (www.diamondbookshelf.com/Home/1/1/20/182?articleID=74165). And when teachers effectively guide students through a read-aloud text, it enhances students' enjoyment and increases their comprehension. Reading aloud, according to Gutierrez, allows teachers to make obvious for students the humor, craft, and subtlety of a graphic novel, as well as how the print and images each support the reading of the other.

Indeed, it's this rich connection that enables graphic narratives in the disciplines to provide unique ways of building knowledge and literacy skills. Yet we cannot expect these skills to develop through the sheer act of reading a comic or graphic novel aloud. The realization of the full literacy- and knowledge-building benefits requires some facilitative strategies that are specific to graphic novels.

Martin, a 10th-grade English teacher, does just that in employing the simplest of systems of working with graphic novels in the classroom. He and his students read aloud graphic novels that are thematically linked to the stories, plays, novels, essays, and poems from their literature anthology.

When Martin's class is reading and analyzing Shakespeare's *Julius Caesar* from their literature book, they also read aloud from two graphic novel versions of the play. One is a more traditional rendition (Bowen & Garcia, 2012); the other, a manga adaptation (Appignanesi & Mustashrik, 2008). The class reads the graphic novels at the same pace as the play so as to compare the texts and have visual references for the words, stage direction, and dialogue.

Martin is able to obtain the Bowen and Garcia version of *Julius Caesar* from his school's librarian, who has provided regular assistance with titles and alternative resources for his units. Adhering closely to the original setting and time period, this graphic novel recounts the epic tale of Julius Caesar's rule over Rome. In detailed and colorful drawings and relying on the authentic language from Shakespeare, the authors show how Caesar grows arrogant after his military victory and falsely assumes the people will hail him as emperor. But staunch republicans Brutus and Cassius assassinate him, ushering in civil war and Antony and Octavius's revenge.

Martin finds the manga edition at www.mangashakespeare.com, where virtually all of the Bard's plays are available. In this powerful adaptation, Mustashrik's distinct and suggestive style makes this tragedy even weightier and more menacing, such as the serpent in Brutus's home and the puppets in Cassius's hands. These touches add depth and layers of meaning to the text, and the artist's rendition of faces accurately captures each character's feelings and emotions. Set in a contemporary world filled with mobile phones and motorcycles, this version of *Caesar* makes it easier for Martin's 15-year-olds to relate to the characters and their motives. Plus, stage directions, included in boxes at the top of panels, help the class follow the action of the story.

As Martin reads, he asks his students to be active listeners, paying attention not only to plot developments but also to how the words and actions in the story relate to the original play in their textbook also being read and discussed. To ensure that all students see the panels and illustrations, Martin projects these on the document camera, capable of reproducing in color. With this approach, only a single copy of a graphic novel is needed. Martin also invites students to read pages and sections aloud from the graphic novels.

Like Martin, Courtney reads aloud from a graphic novel in her high school history and current events classes. For example, to help put a human face on issues relating to the Persian Gulf War, addressed in a typically superficial way in the textbook, Courtney reads *Shooters* (Jerwa, Trautmann, & Lieber, 2012). In this honest and compelling story, a Persian Gulf War veteran returns home to his wife and daughter an emotionally broken man after his involvement in a friendly fire incident. Seeking redemption, he returns to Iraq as a private military contractor.

As a prelude to reading aloud to students, Courtney identifies good prediction points in *Shooters* where students can speculate on the events described and future scenes they will encounter. Also, Courtney has her students compare and contrast the textbook's perspective on the war with that of the graphic novel. Students take positions and debate each other over the issues. Activities like these help her students gain a deeper appreciation and understanding of the topic as well as get a feel for what regular people experienced and how they really felt at that time. By reading aloud for about 10 to 15 minutes at the end of a period from books like *Shooters*, Courtney enriches and keeps her students engaged in content learning.

A Single Graphic Novel for the Whole Class

As an alternative to the teacher or individual students reading aloud from one or two books, the whole class can read or explore a graphic novel together. Although this approach creates more opportunities for students to encounter print, teachers who seek to put a graphic novel in each student's hands are confronted with logistical challenges not present with the methods employed by Martin. The first is finding multiple copies of one title at a reasonable cost to supply one for every student.

Louisa, an 8th-grade science teacher, applies for a small grant from her district's education foundation and is awarded $250 to purchase graphic novels for her class. The premise of her grant is that these alternative texts are more engaging and accessible to her ESOL (English for Speakers of Other Languages) students, who constitute nearly one-third of the total she has in all her science sections.

With the grant money, Louisa is able to buy a class set of *Dynamic World of Chemical Reactions with Max Axiom* (Biskup, 2011). The graphic novel is written in a story format, with textbook features that include a table of contents, a glossary, and suggestions for further reading. The main character is Max Axiom (who appears in a series of STEM-related graphic novels, one of which is referred to earlier in this chapter), an African American scientist working in an innovative laboratory, and just the kind of character who could make the science of chemical reactions interesting for her students.

Louisa's primary reason for using the graphic novel for the unit on chemical reactions is to help students, especially her English language learners, develop a deep understanding of the new key science vocabulary and to reinforce familiar science words. The drawings in the novel are vivid, and the vocabulary-rich text is broken into frames and supported by insets that reinforce vocabulary found in the science textbook and help her students build important schema for the topic.

Multiple Groups and Multiple Graphic Novels

A more complex but exciting and powerful approach involves clusters of students reading and sharing multiple graphic novels that are tied together by the unit's theme. Each cluster of students, say four to five, might operate as literature circles or cooperative groups, or function according to some other process. Regardless of what they're called, the goal for each group and for the whole class is the same—reading, analyzing, and sharing information and ideas from each of their assigned graphic novels.

Debbie, the 8th-grade social studies teacher, employs a multitext/multigroup system during her unit on the American Civil War. As we described earlier, Debbie first decides on a theme for the unit; this is followed by the creation of a topic/subtopic web based on content standards and textbook content; next, she identifies graphic novels that can be incorporated into the unit of study to help engage her students and enrich their understanding of the content; finally, Debbie decides which topics she needs to devote more instructional time to and which can be covered more briskly. In this final step, she decides to stress topics related to slavery and Abraham Lincoln, as they are more closely related to the unit's theme.

With the assistance of her school librarian, Debbie acquires small sets of four graphic novels: *Abraham Lincoln: From the Log Cabin to the White House* (Helfand & Manikandan, 2013); *Harriet Tubman and the Underground Railroad* (Martin & Anderson, 2005); *Slavery's Storm* (Boyd, 2003); and *The Hammer and the Anvil: Frederick Douglass, Abraham Lincoln, and the End of Slavery in America* (Zimmerman & Vansant, 2012). For the 20 students in one of her sections, Debbie creates five groups of four, with three groups assigned one of the four graphic novels while two additional groups are both assigned the Zimmerman and Vansant book, as that is longer and more complex than the others.

Debbie assigns students in each group particular roles to play in order to ensure everyone's participation. The "idea summarizer" is responsible for putting on paper the key information gleaned from the source; the "vocabulary enricher" looks up and helps define unfamiliar words encountered in the source; the "fact-checker" has to find an independent corroborative source for any facts used in the presentation; and the "presenter" is responsible for sharing with the entire class the key ideas and information learned from studying the source.

Once the students are in groups with roles assigned, Debbie begins by modeling the process and expectations for the groups. Since her students are used to working with partners and in other social configurations, they can follow their teacher's directions more readily than students who are less experienced learning together. She carefully models each cooperative group assignment and helps clarify confusion through questions and discussions. She devises these cooperative learning group roles because they contribute to students' learning in the manner she desires and with the graphic novels from which she wants her students to learn. It is important to note that depending on what kinds of learning Debbie expects of students within the groups, she modifies cooperative learning roles accordingly. This system used by Debbie is admirably suited to teaching units because a variety of graphic novels, each emphasizing a different aspect of the unit theme, enriches the scope and depth of students' understanding (Brozo & Simpson, 2007).

In the final section of this chapter, we present important general guidelines for ensuring that students read and engage with graphic novels in appropriate ways. We also share a useful set of criteria for deciding on the best graphic novels to incorporate into disciplinary instruction.

ENSURING STUDENT SUCCESS

The teacher think-aloud is an instruction strategy often recommended for teaching students how to read a text. Think-aloud is a form of modeling in which a proficient reader (the teacher) reads aloud a text and simultaneously shares what she is thinking in a conversational manner. Research demonstrates that this technique improves students' ability to comprehend text (Fisher, Frey, & Lapp, 2011). In the case of graphic novels, the teacher would read a graphic novel aloud (preferably making the pages visible through technology), illustrating how she uses the various graphic elements to make sense of and analyze the text. Using the think-aloud also provides the teacher with the opportunity to integrate the key vocabulary of the graphic novel in an authentic manner. By modeling and sharing her thoughts, the teacher makes an invisible process visible while explicitly teaching the skills necessary to navigate a graphic novel.

As you continue to explore various ways to integrate graphic novels into your instruction, you will no doubt be in search of high-quality and academically appropriate graphic novels. In the following section, we will provide tips for identifying potential graphic novels as well as a checklist to help you select high-quality graphic novels.

Tips for Identifying Potential Graphic Novels

- Review your curriculum to identify potential connections between the curriculum and graphic novels.
- Think about potential instructional uses (whole-group, cooperative groups, and independent study).
- Talk with professionals who are already familiar with the genre. Colleagues, school media specialists, local book and comic book store staff, and public librarians are excellent resources.
- Read reviews and recommendations found on both professional and retailer websites.
- If you opt to use a graphic novel with mature content (like *The 9/11 Report: A Graphic Adaptation* [Jacobson & Colón, 2006]), be prepared to provide a rationale for using the novel to share with administrators and parents. Additionally, allot class time to discuss the responsibility that comes with reading mature content with your students. A very

helpful resource with information on ways to build a case for quality books with content that parents and others may find objectionable can be found in *Keep Them Reading: An Anti-Censorship Handbook for Educators* (Lent & Pipkin, 2013).

• Finally and most importantly, please remember that authors and illustrators create graphic novels for diverse audiences ranging from preschool children to adults. Always read the entire graphic novel to ensure that it is developmentally appropriate for your students.

Once you identify graphic novels with potential instructional use, you will need to evaluate them to ensure that they are of sufficient quality to deserve a place in your instruction. When evaluating graphic novels, you must consider the artwork, the format, the content, the text, and the text's developmental appropriateness. The following checklist (Figure 2.3) can help you determine whether or not a particular graphic novel should be used in your classroom.

When integrating graphic novels into your instruction, it is essential to identify graphic novels that not only motivate and engage your students but also introduce your students to high-quality texts appropriate in a secondary classroom. We believe that using the tips and checklist included in this section provide guidance in your quest to develop authentic content instruction using graphic novels.

LOOKING BACK AND MOVING FORWARD

This chapter presented several important guidelines for identifying and teaching with graphic novels. The guidelines are intended to make teaching and learning in the disciplines more effective and are based on concerns about (1) student engagement, (2) student diversity, (3) managing instruction with graphic novels, (4) building disciplinary knowledge through reading and writing, and (5) ensuring selection of the best possible graphic novels for supporting student learning.

Six disciplinary teachers with differing approaches to integrating graphic novels into their classroom routines were described in this chapter in order to demonstrate the instructional possibilities and management considerations of using this versatile resource. Whether reading aloud from a single copy of a graphic novel, providing students with their own copies of a single title, or orchestrating the simultaneous exploration of multiple graphic novels by groups of students, subject area teachers have discovered numerous ways to ensure that their students have encounters with content in the disciplines through this unique text.

As alternatives and supplements to traditional textbooks, graphic novels have many advantages that a growing number of teachers are recognizing. In

Figure 2.3. Checklist for Adopting Graphic Novels

Consideration	Yes or No?	Additional Thoughts
Artwork		
Does the cover art appeal to the target audience?		
Does the cover art distinctly convey the theme/topic of the book?		
Is the artwork appropriate for the target audience?		
Does the artwork align with the story?		
Does the use of color scaffold the readers understanding of the mood and tone of the story?		
Is the artwork of adequate size?		
Text		
Do the word balloons contain an appropriate number of words?		
Do the artwork and text work in tandem?		
Do the tone of the artwork and the tone of the text match?		
Is the reading level appropriate for the intended audience?		
Does the text include traditional elements such as plot, theme, setting, etc.?		
Are the main characters developed with their own voices?		
Is the information presented in the text accurate and relevant?		
Format and Structure		
Does the panel arrangement scaffold readers' understanding?		
Do the panels enhance the story?		
Do the gutters aid comprehension?		
Are the pages clear and easy to understand?		
Within the panel, is the text readable?		

subsequent chapters, several teachers from the four major disciplines, English/
language arts, history, science, and math, are described employing innovative
and engaging instructional practices with graphic novels. Using these approaches, the teachers have energized their own instruction while increasing student
interest and learning.

Study Group Questions for Chapter 2

- Does your school library have a substantial collection of graphic
  novels? Does it have graphic novels that could be used in different
  disciplines? If not, what can you and your colleagues do to acquire
  additional titles for use in a variety of subject areas?

- Work with colleagues to create a topic/subtopic web for an upcoming
  unit. Afterward, conduct research with the help of your school
  librarian to identify possible graphic novels that might be used to
  teach the topics and subtopics of the unit.

- What hurdles do you envision in trying to integrate graphic novels
  into the disciplinary curriculum at your school? How could these
  hurdles be overcome?

CHAPTER THREE

Using Graphic Novels to Teach English and the Language Arts

ANTICIPATION GUIDE

Directions: Read each statement carefully and decide whether you agree or disagree with it, placing a check mark in the appropriate Before Reading column. When you have finished reading and studying Chapter 3, return to the guide and decide whether your anticipations need to be changed by placing a check mark in the appropriate After Reading column.

	BEFORE READING		AFTER READING	
	Agree	*Disagree*	*Agree*	*Disagree*
1. Graphic novels are high-quality literature.				
2. Graphic novels should be used solely with struggling and/or reluctant readers.				
3. Literacy in the 21st century requires more than the ability to read and write printed text.				
4. Graphic novels can help develop students' enthusiasm for classic literature.				
5. Graphic novels can be used to teach traditional literary themes.				

Romeo and Juliet is one of Shakespeare's most dynamic and powerful plays. It is commonly part of the curriculum in secondary schools. However, most high school students find the prose difficult, if not completely incomprehensible. These panels include two well-known quotes ("O Romeo, Romeo, wherefore art thou, Romeo?" and "That which we call a rose by any other word would smell as sweet") and demonstrates how graphic art can bring life to the script.

If you acquire graphic novels, young adults will come.

—Maureen Mooney,
Graphic Novels: How They Can Work in Libraries

AS HAS BEEN THE CASE WITH many new genres, acceptance of graphic novels in literary circles has been slow. For example, a new written form appeared in the late 1700s that critics claimed misled readers into false impressions of reality, and presented false and potentially damaging perspectives on personal, social, and cultural issues. The genre? The novel (Hansen, 2012). More recently, comic books, the predecessor of the graphic novel, were the target of attacks during the 1940s and 1950s. In *Seduction of the Innocent,* published in 1954, Dr. Fredrick Wertham, a prominent psychologist, claimed that comic books were a major cause of juvenile delinquency, taught erroneous scientific concepts, encouraged homosexuality, and provided girls with poor role models (Coville, 2013). In general during this time, educators believed that comic books interfered with students' literacy growth.

Over time, literary scholars and English educators have come to view comics and, more recently, graphic novels as worthy and valuable texts. As evidence of their quality, graphic novels have won literary awards traditionally reserved for nonillustrated books, including the Pulitzer Prize, the Hugo Award, the Guardian First Book Award, and the World Fantasy Award. Professional organizations such as the ALA, NCTE, and IRA support their instructional use and provide updated lists of quality graphic novels. Libraries report growing circulation: In a report in *Publishers Weekly* (MacDonald, 2013), one county library in Ohio reported that graphic novels made up 10% of its collection but 35% of its circulation, and a junior high school library in Brooklyn reported that graphic novels are 3% of its holdings and 30% of its circulation. Perhaps the most compelling sign of the worthiness of graphic novels is their enormous popularity among today's adolescents.

Graphic novels, and before them comic books, first found their way into the English/language arts (ELA) classroom as a teaching tool for struggling or reluctant readers. Graphics combined with text made both decoding text and comprehending story or information easier and provided a bridge for dealing with nonillustrated text. While the research base is currently limited, there is reasonable evidence that graphic novels

- Motivate reluctant readers
- Provide assistance for struggling readers
- Foster visual literacy
- Support English language learners

There is a danger, however, in concentrating on the use of graphic novels as remedial texts. Too often, graphic novels are viewed as less sophisticated, easier reading material. This is clearly an outdated and false perception that fails to recognize the high literary and aesthetic quality of the body of graphic novel literature. We argue that graphic novels are the equal of other forms of literature in terms of interest, complexity, and academic quality. In this chapter we will demonstrate how graphic novels can be used to address the traditional goals of ELA instruction.

Graphic novels are potentially transformative, providing teachers with a tool to break the common pattern in English classrooms of students reading only long enough and deeply enough to get a desired grade (Bakis, 2013). This pattern denies students the joy of thoughtful, leisurely, and enlightening reading. And it denies both teachers and students the exciting conversations that grow out of such readings. Reading graphic novels requires the reader to slow down, to reread, to analyze both text and pictures in order to construct an understanding of the narrative. This form of reading text that includes two or more media has been termed *multimodal literacy*.

Multimodal literacy requires combining information from multiple sources in order to comprehend (in the case of reading) or to construct (in the case of writing) a text. Text, from this perspective, takes on a broader meaning and includes such things as film, television, graphics, and the Internet. Today's adolescents live in a multimodal environment outside of school, acting regularly and effectively with multimodal texts. As educators, we can help prepare our students for success in college and the workplace by enhancing this more complex form of literacy. So it is that when the need to teach new skills becomes evident, the tools to do so appear. Graphic novels are one, quite strong method that can be utilized to help students become multimodal literate.

Graphic novels have the potential to teach character development, dialogue, symbolism, foreshadowing, and other traditional literary concepts. In addition, they can improve multimodal literacy. In this chapter we will illustrate how graphic novels can be incorporated into the regular ELA curriculum, both as supplemental texts to more traditional literature and as stand-alone texts.

INSTRUCTIONAL PRACTICES WITH GRAPHIC NOVELS IN ENGLISH/LANGUAGE ARTS

ELA teachers should bring graphic novels into the classroom in a thoughtful and systematic manner. There is no need to engage in some form of radical pedagogy. For the most part, graphic novel instruction involves the same principles used with any sort of text: Learning principles, teaching methods and strategies, classroom management, and goals of instruction remain the same. In this section, we will illustrate how three teachers integrated graphic novels into their existing curriculum. In the first lesson, Susan uses a single graphic novel that she reads aloud to the class to teach traditional legends. In the second, Trevor provides all his students with a copy of a graphic novel version of *Romeo and Juliet*. In the final example, Meredith creates book clubs that read four different graphic novels centered around the study of literary themes.

Using Graphic Novels to Teach Traditional Legends

Susan teaches 7th-grade ELA in a rural elementary school. Her students are culturally and racially diverse, with a wide range of reading abilities and interests. Susan loves literature, particularly traditional British literature. She is required to use the adopted literature anthology, *Elements of Literature* (Holt, Rinehart and Winston, 2006). She finds the textbook both helpful and limiting. While it provides structure both within her class and across grade levels, it does not always have the kinds of reading selections that she would chose. One exception is a classic rendition of the legend *King Arthur: The Sword in the Stone*. In the past, however, she has found that even her more skilled readers struggle with the text, and most do not find the story relevant or interesting.

As an undergraduate teacher education student several years earlier, Susan had been introduced to graphic novels in a children's literature class. One of her favorites was *Beowulf* by Gareth Hinds (2007). In the middle of the night, Susan awakes with the sudden vision of combining the two stories. She believes that reading aloud the colorful and highly engaging *Beowulf* will motivate her students for the interesting but hard to read *King Arthur: The Sword in the Stone*.

Susan begins preparation for the lesson by carefully rereading *Beowulf*. To make herself comfortable with the oral readings she plans to do, Susan finds an isolated room in the school and reads each of the *Beowulf* chapters aloud. She pays attention to the brief historical account at the beginning: an epic poem of events that probably took place around 500 A.D., passed down orally over many generations before the first written manuscript appeared around 1000. She determines that this version of the legend is divided into three books; note that we will refer to these three books as chapters to avoid confusion. Believing that her students, especially the boys, will find the adventure and violence very alluring, she searches the Internet for additional information. She finds an enormous amount of quality information, for example:

- Summaries of the plot, including an outstanding video on YouTube.
- Character analysis, including a very readable text at www.csis.pace. edu/grendel/projf981e/char.html.
- Several trailers for movie versions of *Beowulf*, also on YouTube.

Next Susan turns her attention to reviewing the anthology's teacher's edition. She learns that the focus skill is analyzing legends and that the text is rated as above grade level in reading difficulty. She makes notes on the background information provided that she thinks will be useful to pass along to her students. For example, the King Arthur legends contain a little fact and a lot of story. Although King Arthur and most of the characters were real people who lived sometime around 500 A.D., the minstrel who originally told the story cared more about entertainment than facts. In reviewing the instructional suggestions, she finds that the teacher's manual offers far more suggestions than can possibly be implemented. In addition, she notes places where she thinks her students will need additional instruction not specified in the teacher's edition. As with *Beowulf,* Susan is certain that her students will want more information on King Arthur. By doing a basic Internet search she finds these resources:

- An outstanding website, King Arthur and the Knights of the Round Table (www.kingarthursknights.com/).
- A YouTube video of the 2004 Antoine Fuqua film
- A historical account, *King Arthur: The History, the Legend, the King* (www.britannia.com/history/h12.html)

Susan thinks it is critical that her students become actively engaged in dialogue about the legend. She decides to utilize the Think-Pair-Share strategy (Reading Quest, 2013) to engage students in postreading discussions. In this strategy students are given a question or prompt and a limited amount of time to think through the question. Then they discuss their thoughts with a partner. Finally, the teacher calls on partners to share their thinking with the whole class. Susan thinks that two higher-order questions or prompts will sustain a lively discussion after each oral reading. Therefore, she constructs these questions:

Chapter One

- Why do you think Beowulf wanted to destroy Grendel?
- The fight between Beowulf and Grendel is not described in words. Describe it.

Chapter Two

- What were the consequences of Beowulf mortally wounding Grendel, and then hanging his severed arm from the gable on the roof?
- What were the consequences of Beowulf killing Grendel's mother?

Chapter Three

- What did you think when Beowulf's comrades said, "Foul shame it were if we should carry back our shields to our home unless we can first destroy the enemy and save our King"?
- Write an obituary for Beowulf.

Susan is now ready to begin the lesson. To grab the students' attention and interest, she begins by showing the trailer to the 2007 movie version of *Beowulf* she found on YouTube. She then reads the first of the three *Beowulf* chapters using her smart board to project the book onto the screen. Because of her earlier practice reading aloud, she reads enthusiastically and fluently. She spends time discussing the interesting graphics and engages the students in discussions about how the pictures and text combine to create meaning in the story. She pays special attention to the graphics in the novel. Since they carry a great deal of the narrative and there are many consecutive pages without written text, she views this as an opportunity to enhance students' visual literacy skills.

When she has finished the first chapter, she puts the two Think-Pair-Share prompts up on the smart board and instructs the students to think about how they can respond. After about 5 minutes she allows her students to self-select partners for the activity, then instructs them to spend 10 minutes in discussion with their partner. As students talk, she circulates among the partners, clarifying her expectations and encouraging them to be thoughtful and creative. At the end of 10 minutes she asks for volunteers to report on their conversations. She also encourages nonresponsive pairs to add their thoughts to the larger discussion.

After the discussion, Susan debriefs the students about the day's activities. First she asks students about the Think-Pair-Share strategy. For the most part, students are enthusiastic about the opportunity to share their thoughts about the graphic novel. They comment that, in their experience, classroom discussions for the most part have included only a few of the most assertive students and consist more of the teacher talking than students talking. Susan also asks about the graphic novel. The boys in her class are for the most part more enthusiastic about the book than are the girls. The boys like the action and the violence. The girls seem to enjoy the artwork and think the story is interesting. Overall, Susan decides she was on the right track with her planning and decides to continue with the read-aloud. Over the next two classes, she reads chapters 2 and 3 and engages the students in the Think-Pair-Share activity.

The final Think-Pair-Share prompt (asking students to write an obituary for Beowulf) turns out to be a perfect end to the read-aloud portion of the lesson. In their pairs, students write out their obituaries, then read them aloud to the class. The obituaries serve as an informal assessment of how well the students understand the Beowulf legend. Susan believes they are strong evidence that the graphic novel was well understood and that her students gained perspective on traditional legends as well as skill at combining text and artwork to understand narrative.

The obituaries also initiate an engaging discussion that leads to an overview of the King Arthur legend. Susan begins this overview by asking students to predict how Beowulf and King Arthur are both alike and different. This brainstorming activity serves as the framework for filling in students' background knowledge before they begin reading the text in the anthology. Susan will then engage the students in a guided reading lesson, following, with many adaptations, the lessons as they are outlined in the teacher's edition.

Using a Graphic Novel Version of *Romeo and Juliet*

Trevor teaches high school English in a suburban school. For academic classes students are tracked into groups based on performance on the previous year's end-of-course tests. One of his favorite classes is a freshman-level class of midperformance students. He has taught and developed this class over a 5-year period but is still not satisfied with it. The class meets for 90 minutes three times a week. Part of the curriculum in his school and state is to teach Shakespeare, and the play of choice is *Romeo and Juliet*. Each year he looks forward to teaching the play with mixed emotions. Like most English teachers, he loves Shakespeare and believes that *Romeo and Juliet* is particularly relevant for adolescents. However, even his best students struggle with the complex and unfamiliar language.

In a professional development workshop, Trevor is introduced to graphic novels. In his exploration of the genre, he discovers that many of Shakespeare's plays have been rewritten as graphic novels. Trevor sees the potential of illustrated versions of the plays. By coincidence, some extra money appears in his department budget, giving him a windfall budget of $500. Searching online and in a local bookstore, Trevor finds *Romeo and Juliet, the Graphic Novel* (McDonald & Shakespeare, 2009). Using his budget, he purchases a class set of 30 books.

The graphic novel addresses one of the problems in teaching *Romeo and Juliet*: Shakespeare never intended his plays to be read but, rather, viewed. In past years, Trevor experimented with showing the 1996 film version directed by Baz Luhrmann, starring Leonardo DiCaprio and Claire Danes and set in a fictionalized modern city. He found that showing the film increases student interest but that most of his students still struggle with reading, understanding, and relating to this masterpiece. An Internet search locates a YouTube trailer of the film he thinks will be useful.

Trevor has participated in numerous plays, in high school, college, and the local community theater. He knows that another way to enhance the experience of any play is to act in it. As a dedicated reader of the professional literature,

Trevor is familiar with the teaching strategy of reader's theater. An article in *The Reading Teacher* (Worthy & Prater, 2002) convinced him that this technique could be applied to Shakespeare and would help his students see how the play could be applied to their own lives. Reader's theater puts students in the roles of writer, actor, and producer. Trevor minimizes his students' role as writers, using the original script as written in the literature anthology he uses (EMC, 2005). But he will help them become actors and producers.

As Trevor begins to plan for the unit on *Romeo and Juliet,* he is determined to utilize these features: the graphic novel version of the play, the trailer and full version of the Luhrmann film, and reader's theater. A vision of the unit is beginning to form, but one more piece of background work needs to be done. Knowing that the reader's theater will require a list of actors for each act, Trevor does an Internet search to see if he can get some help. Using the terms "Romeo and Juliet Characters," he finds a site that lists the characters by scene. He adapts this list to present the characters by act, which suits his evolving plan. From the list he develops the handout shown in Figure 3.1.

Trevor now feels that he is prepared to initiate the unit. He believes the well-thought-out plans allow him to make changes as he goes, to adapt the instruction to the needs of the students and take advantage of teachable moments. He

Figure 3.1. Characters in Shakespeare's *Romeo and Juliet*

ACT 1

Chorus, Sampson, Gregory, Abram, Balthasar, Benvolio, Tybalt, Citizens, Montague, Lady Montague, Prince Escalus, Romeo, Capulet, County Paris, Second Servingman, Lady Capulet, Nurse, Juliet, First Servingman, Mercutio, Maskers, Torch-Bearers, Anthony, Potpan, Old Capulet, Guests, Gentlewomen

ACT 2

Chorus, Romeo, Benvolio, Mercutio, Juliet, Nurse, Friar Lawrence, Peter

ACT 3

Mercutio, Benvolio, Page, Men, Tybalt, Petruchio, Romeo, Citizens, Prince Escalus, Montague, Capulet, Lady Capulet, Lady Montague, Juliet, Nurse, Friar Lawrence

ACT 4

Friar Lawrence, County Paris, Juliet, Capulet, Lady Capulet, Nurse, Servingmen, Musicians, Peter

ACT 5

Romeo, Balthasar, Apothecary, Friar John, Friar Lawrence, Page, Juliet, Boy, Watchmen, Prince Escalus, Attendants, Montague carefully plans for 4 weeks of instruction, which will culminate in his students performing *Romeo and Juliet*.

Day One. The first day is busy as Trevor sets the stage for the unit. He explains to the students that they will become actors in one of the most famous plays of all time and provides background on the life and times of Shakespeare. He gives a brief explanation of reader's theater and then plays the YouTube video of the movie trailer. Each student is given a copy of *Romeo and Juliet, the Graphic Novel* and instructed to take 5 minutes to look through the book. At the end of the 5 minutes, Trevor elicits and answers all questions the students have.

He then initiates the cooperative groups. In his planning Trevor had carefully assigned students to groups so that each group was diverse in terms of gender, achievement, and academic enthusiasm. He has avoided placing either close friends or adversaries in the same group. Trevor makes explicit his expectations for behavior in the cooperative groups. Students are given a short time to socialize within the groups.

As class draws toward an end, Trevor provides a general overview of the unit. The culminating activity of performing the play is met with mixed reactions. The quieter students are apprehensive, but many of the students are excited about the idea. Next, Trevor previews, then assigns, Act One in the graphic novel for homework and tells students to be sure to bring both their literature anthologies and *Romeo and Juliet* graphic novels to class each day throughout the unit. He emphasizes the importance of reading each act as assigned. With the short amount of time remaining, he allows students to begin reading Act One.

Day Two: Class begins with Trevor answering all questions students have. He is careful to emphasize the importance of the artwork in the book and encourages students to analyze how the graphics enhance their understanding of the play. Trevor explains that the groups will rotate two leadership roles. He then instructs students to elect leaders for the first act: Role One is the spokesperson, who will speak for the group in the whole-class discussions that will follow reader's theater; Role Two is the actor allocator, who will lead the process of assigning a character or characters to each group member. Trevor then passes out the "Characters in *Romeo and Juliet*" handout and explains that the process should be based as much as possible on what role each member wants. Students are given the opportunity to ask questions, then told to get into groups and begin reader's theater. Students must use their literature anthologies, since the characters in the graphic novel are not clearly labeled.

During reader's theater Trevor circulates among the groups and provides instruction and assistance as appropriate. Several times he halts all groups to provide instructions in the common interest. When there are 15 minutes left in class, he stops the reader's theater and asks each spokesperson to report on the group's experience. The students' reports are brief and not very descriptive. This part of the lesson does not go well at first, but with Trevor's direction the dialogue moves along. This is something that he had anticipated, so he is prepared to provide additional instruction on how to discuss group activity. He explains how the groups can encourage participation of all members and provides guidelines for what to do if the group finishes early or fails to finish before the end of class. Trevor concludes the day with a preview and time to begin reading Act Two in the graphic novel.

Days Three–Six: Trevor continues reader's theater following the same format from Day Two. Refinements are made daily. Students are instructed to alternate the two roles; if possible, every student should serve in each role, and no student should serve twice until all students have participated. Trevor monitors student contributions within each group and encourages the shyer students while reminding the more outgoing students to allow everyone to participate. He begins to query students about whether they would like an audience for the final production of the play. If so, who should be invited? Would they rather do a video? Would they like to do both?

Day Seven: Trevor informs students that the next activity is the production of the final play. Each of the five groups will work on one act. The groups draw numbers (1–5); the group that draws number one gets first pick of which act they want to perform. Trevor emphasizes that they are responsible for a "production," not just reading the play. He encourages creativity and getting into the characters. Students then get into their cooperative groups with instructions to assign characters, brainstorm the production (props, movement, placement, etc.), and begin to practice reading the parts.

Day Eight: This is a serious workday. Trevor circulates among the groups, providing assistance as needed. Trevor decides at this point that students will need an additional workday to successfully perform the play. When he announces this, students cheer.

Day Nine: Additional workday for students.

Day Ten: Performance day! Based on ongoing discussions with the students, Trevor has invited parents, administrators, and elders from a local assisted living facility. Initially quite nervous, students give an outstanding performance. Resounding applause at the end brings smiles of pride and joy to the students' faces.

Days Eleven and Twelve: As a culminating activity, Trevor shows the Luhrmann (1996) film version, *Romeo + Juliet*. He divides the 2-hour film into two parts, approximately 1 hour each. He uses the last 30 minutes of each 90-minute period to discuss the play and the students' experience with reader's theater.

Trevor uses the discussions to evaluate the impact of the instruction. He is interested in how students value both the graphic novel and reader's theater as learning activities. Student comments are clear. Reading the graphic novel made the play easily understandable despite the difficult language. Combining acting out the play with the graphic novel gave them great insight into Shakespeare's genius. When Trevor asks if they would like to read more graphic novels, the answer is a resounding yes.

Trevor knows from his own early experiences as a student that reading Shakespeare is a daunting task. From his experience as a teacher, he recognizes that students struggle with both the reading and the relevance of the plays. He is convinced that the enhanced instruction he developed for the *Romeo and Juliet* lesson was successful in engaging his students in one of the classic works in all of Western literature. Trevor is also impressed with the students' enthusiasm for the graphic novel and intends to look for additional ways to include the genre in his instruction.

Using Graphic Novels to Explore Literary Themes

Meredith teaches English in an urban school with a very diverse student population, including ethnic minorities and English language learners. She has become adept at making alterations in the literature anthology she is required to follow. *Prentice Hall Literature: The American Experience* (Pearson Prentice Hall, 2007) is the text for her 11th-grade class. She finds one of the themes she must teach toward the end of the year a paradox: *Literature confronts the everyday*. She knows from past experience that the readings in the anthology are too difficult for most of her students and have little appeal to any of them. With the blessings of an enlightened principal, she sets about to create an alternative set of readings using graphic novels to produce a summative unit in which students explore the struggles humans face in life.

Meredith begins planning for the unit by seeking the help of the school media specialist, Kathy. With the purpose of the unit in mind, Meredith and Kathy work to identify appropriate graphic novels. They hope to find graphic novels with topics that not only appeal to the students but that also have stories that provide the literary weight for the students to critically read and analyze the text. Finally, after meeting for several hours after school for a week, Meredith and Kathy identify four graphic novels they believe provide both the literary weight and relevant topics needed to make the unit a success: *A Contract with God and Other Tenement Stories*

(Eisner, 2006), *A.D.: New Orleans After the Deluge* (Neufeld, 2010), *Yummy: The Last Days of a Southside Shorty* (Neri, 2010), and *Bayou, Volume 1* (Love, 2009).

Ever resourceful, Meredith and Kathy contact a local arts council that will provide grant monies to local classroom teachers who integrate the visual arts into their instruction. Excited by the possibilities, Meredith and Kathy discuss additional avenues to integrate visual literacy into the unit. The pair identifies several online sites that would allow the students to create their own digital panels. After reading reviews on the various free sites, Meredith and Kathy opt to use Toondoo (www.toondoo.com) for the project. The partners prepare a proposal for the arts council. After a few days, they are thrilled to learn that the council has agreed to cover the cost of the books.

With books in hand, Meredith begins to plan the unit. She intends to use instructional book clubs that will allow small groups of student to discuss common books both in and outside of class (Seyfried, 2008). Meredith believes that having choices is a great motivator for her students and will introduce the books through book talks. She will allow students input when assigning students to a book. Because graphic novels are new to many of her students, she decides to use a familiar resource, the students' writing notebooks, to support her students' reading of the graphic novels. Next, Meredith searches the Internet for a list of most common themes found in literature. After exploring various websites, she identifies the three themes on which the unit will focus:

1. Humankind's struggles with nature;
2. Humankind's struggles with society; and
3. Humankind's struggle to understand the Divine.

Meredith plans to complete the majority of the unit during class time. The English class meets on a daily basis for 45 minutes, so she decides to allot 8 days. On the first day, as students walk into class, Meredith projects a page from *A.D.: New Orleans After the Deluge* using a document camera. She engages the students in a discussion about the format. She thinks aloud as she makes sense of the page using terminology she expects her students to learn during the unit. After introducing the format of graphic novels to the class, she uses the rest of the time to introduce each novel through a book talk.

Book Talk One: *A Contract with God*. This revolutionary book by Will Eisner (2006) is usually credited with being the first time the term *graphic novel* and an actual book came together (Kan, 2010). Originally published in 1978, this book provided credibility for adult-level illustrated books. Eisner is one of the most respected graphic novel artists. Born in 1917, he was an early pioneer in comics and other forms of sequential art. In 1940, he created the comic character the Spirit that appeared weekly in newspapers nationwide, reaching an audience of 5 million readers. In 1988, the comic industry created the Eisner Award, which Eisner himself won several times. Clearly one of the most influential artists of our time, Eisner died in 2005.

A Contract with God is actually a collection of four stories set in the Bronx, one of the five boroughs of New York City, during the 1930s. For our book clubs we will be reading only the first, which is also titled "A Contract with God." The book follows the life of Frimme Hersh. Born in Russia in 1881, Frimme is sent by the elders of his village to America to avoid the slaughter of Jews taking place at the time. On his journey he makes a "contract with God," devoting himself to good works. Seemingly favored by fate, he prospers in the Jewish community in his new home. Then one day his adopted daughter dies, leaving Frimme to believe that God has broken the contract. He leaves his pious life to become a rich but amoral man. How the rest of his life and his death play out will present the reader with thought-provoking moral dilemmas that will lead the book club into many interesting discussions.

Book Talk Two: *A.D.: New Orleans After the Deluge.* On August 29, 2005, Hurricane Katrina struck the Gulf Coast of the United States. Rated a category 3 hurricane, it brought winds of 100 to 140 miles per hour and was 400 miles across. While the initial storm did considerable damage, the flooding that followed was even more devastating. New Orleans was particularly hard hit. Between the rains, the storm surge, and the failure of the city's unstable levee system, 80% of the city was under water. In some areas the water was 15 feet deep and people fled to rooftops to avoid drowning. While nearly 400,000 of the city's 500,000 residents evacuated the city before Katrina hit, the aftermath of the storm left New Orleans in chaos. Many of those left behind were elderly or sick. And to add to the catastrophe, the federal government was slow to recognize the severity of the problem and to respond with disaster relief.

A.D.: New Orleans After the Deluge (Neufeld, 2010) provides a personal face for the Katrina story. It follows seven real-life survivors of the storm. The life-and-death decisions that each must make are chronicled within the context of the lackluster response of state and federal officials. The reader will be drawn into the growing desperation of the situation. Many interesting anecdotes provide insight into what happened in the aftermath of the storm. For example, in one interesting scene gang members show up at the Superdome, the designated "shelter of last resort," with lifesaving water, food, and drugs that they have looted from area stores. This disturbing book was nominated for both the Eisner and Harvey awards, two of the most prestigious awards for comics and graphic novels.

Book Talk Three: *Yummy: The Last Days of a Southside Shorty.* On any given day in the United States, turn on the evening news or click on an

Internet news outlet, and you can find a story detailing the latest victim of gun violence in our cities. In particular, gun violence has plagued the South Side of Chicago for decades. Guns and gangs have contributed to Chicago's history of violence from the days of Al Capone and Tommy guns to today's handguns and semi-automatic weapons. Between 2008 and 2011, 286 youth living in Chicago died from gun violence (Lydersen & Ortiz, 2012). Many of the youth living in Chicago turn to gangs and guns for protection, which ironically contributes to continued violence.

Yummy: The Last Days of a Southside Shorty (Neri, 2010) brings names, faces, and a personal story to the violence from which we try distance ourselves. Narrated by 11-year-old Roger, *Yummy* tells the true story of the 1994 Chicago shooting death of 14-year-old Shavon Dean. The story unfolds through Roger's eyes as he struggles to make sense out of the senseless. He tries to understand how and why his 11-year-old classmate Robert "Yummy" Sandifer, known for his love of sweets and carrying a teddy bear, could be involved in such a horrific crime. More importantly, Roger struggles to understand why Yummy joined a violent gang, the same gang Roger's older brother runs with.

Book Talk Four: *Bayou, Volume 1*. From the 1880s until the 1960s, American states, cities, municipalities, and so on could impose laws that forbade people to consort with people of different races (National Park Service, n.d.). The post–Civil War "Black Codes" were more than a series of rigid antiblack laws, they were a way of life (Pilgrim, 2012). Meredith identifies examples of laws from this time using the website. She then prompts partner discussion using the following question: Can you imagine living under these laws? In the South, people of color lived in fear of breaking the codes and were terrorized by the fear of the retribution they would face, both legal and nonlegal.

Bayou, Volume 1 (Love, 2009), a fantasy set in the Jim Crow South, tells the story of two parallel worlds, the Jim Crow South and an alternative world of gods and monsters. The author uses the alternative world of gods and monsters to examine centuries of slavery, hate, and prejudice. Lee Wagstaff, a sharecropper's daughter, is learning to live in the Jim Crow South when a monster from the parallel world abducts Lee's White friend, Lily. Chaos and terror ensue. The White townspeople accuse Lee's father of the kidnapping, and Lee herself is in danger. To save her father, Lee must enter this parallel world of gods and monsters and rescue her friend. Along the way, she meets Bayou, a blues singer monster, who acts as her guide as she navigates the Dixie stereotypes brought to life by the author.

After the book talks are complete, Meredith asks her students to complete an exit pass, a question prompt or activity completed by the students to determine their understanding of a concept, in their writer's notebook and answer the following question: What do all the shared graphic novels have in common? In addition, Meredith asks the students to rate their book choices from first to last. As the students complete their exit passes, they give Meredith their writing notebooks and leave the class. Many of them talk among themselves about the books and the upcoming assignment. During her planning, Meredith creates the book clubs. She wants to place every student in his or her first or second pick and is excited when she can do so. In addition, she reads the students' exit pass responses. She is pleased to see that most students synthesized the information from all four graphic novels and recognized that the characters in the graphic novels all encounter hardships and difficulties in the stories.

On Day Two, Meredith reviews the vocabulary she wants the students to learn and use when discussing graphic novels: (1) panel, (2) frame, (3) gutter, (4) graphic weight, and (5) bleed. She provides a student-friendly explanation of each word and directs students to write the definition in their writing notebooks. Meredith also shares a visual she has created that clarifies the terminology using panels from *Yummy*. She thinks aloud about how she uses the graphic techniques in tandem with the printed text to make sense of the panel. Next Meredith distributes the books to the students. She tells the students they will have 5 days to read and discuss the books in their groups, allowing each group to determine the pace at which the books should be read. She asks each group to write down their pacing goals so she can post the goals on the class calendar. To end class, Meredith presents a mini-lesson on theme. Reading aloud an excerpt from a story read earlier in the year, she thinks aloud about what clues the author provides about the story's theme. Together, she and the class discuss how to determine theme when reading literature. Meredith concludes class by asking her students to complete a quickwrite in their writing journals. The students answer the following question: How do you think determining theme will differ when reading a graphic novel as compared to reading a traditional story?

Meredith designates Day Three as "go day." When the students arrive in class, she has the three unit themes paired with the novel she has selected on the board. She informs students that each of them will independently read their group's assigned pages and are to read like a writer, a phrase she has used throughout the year. It is Meredith's cue that the students are to read critically, paying close attention to the author's choice of words, voice, and so on. Meredith directs the students to pay attention to the theme of their book and to note how the author uses language and the illustrator uses visuals to convey the theme of the book to the reader. She reminds students that authors and illustrators of graphic novels must work in tandem to tell a story. She provides students with 30 minutes to read and take notes in their writing journals. As the students read, Meredith circulates among them. She randomly asks students questions about the text to ensure that students comprehend the text. During this time, the students are engaged in reading quietly and making notes in their writing notebooks.

As students enter on Day Four, Meredith directs them into their reading groups. She provides 10 minutes for the students to discuss the notes taken on the previous day. Meredith requires the groups to come to a consensus and create a master list of techniques the authors and illustrators use to convey theme. The students partake in lively small-group discussions. They share what they have learned while reading independently. Meredith is pleased to see that the students refer to both their notes and to the actual text during their discussions. As the allotted time draws to a close, Meredith checks in with each group to determine their progress. Students use the remaining time to read and take notes. Day Five is a repeat of Day Four; however, Meredith reminds the students that they should conclude their independent reading.

On Day Six, the groups once again meet for 10 minutes to compile a master list of text examples that support the theme of the story. Meredith collects each group's work. She uses the work as a formative assessment to determine whether or not her students can identify text that supports the story's theme. Next, she takes the students to the computer lab. Here she directs the students to visit www.toondoo.com. Using a computer connected to a projector, Meredith demonstrates how to create an account and then how to create panels using this online resource. She provides the remainder of the class time for the students to simply explore and play with the site, so they feel comfortable creating a panel. The students eagerly explore the digital tool. Some students have used the tool previously and help their classmates who have not. Meredith is amazed at how quickly the students learn to effectively use the tool. As an exit pass, each student must show Meredith a panel created during the exploration time. She is quite pleased at her students' efforts. Each student completes a panel, and Meredith notes that students are already using techniques used in graphic novels to help convey their message.

On Day Seven, the students return to the computer lab. At the beginning of class, Meredith explains to the students, they will use *Toondoo* to create panels relating to the graphic novel just read. She instructs the students to keep in mind the theme of the story, and the techniques used by the author and illustrators to convey the theme of the story. Meredith informs the students that the theme of their panels is *Perseverance*. She then tells the students to select a main character from the story and to imagine the character's life 3 years after the story ends, and instructs them to create panels depicting the future life of the character. The students enthusiastically begin working. While the students work, Meredith reminds them that the panels should illustrate the character's perseverance. Throughout the work period, the students refer back to their assigned graphic novels to explore how the author and illustrators used graphic techniques to convey their message.

On the last day, the students share their panels with the class. To wrap up the unit, Meredith asks the students to complete one last exit pass. She asks the students to write a brief entry in their writing notebooks, a reflection about what they have learned from the unit. While reading the students' notebooks, Meredith is pleased to see that many of her students identified two main literary concepts from the unit. First, the students recognize how graphic techniques help to strengthen the author/illustrators' storytelling. In addition, she is thrilled to see her students writing about the importance of theme in literature.

LOOKING BACK AND MOVING FORWARD

In this chapter, we explored the potential of integrating graphic novels into the English/language arts classroom. We shared three approaches used by English teachers in middle and high schools to successfully integrate graphic novels into their instruction. In two classrooms, graphic novels are paired with traditional texts and instructional strategies are used to scaffold a deep understanding of a classic tale and a Shakespearian play. In the third classroom, multiple graphic novels paired with writer's notebook are used to explore literary themes and author's and illustrator's craft. In each classroom, the teachers incorporated graphic novels in a manner that promoted in-depth, engaged learning in the ELA classroom.

In the next chapter, you will meet history teachers who, like the ELA teachers in this chapter, recognize the unique opportunities that graphic novels bring to their discipline. How graphic novels can enhance the social studies curriculum and develop literacy is explored.

Study Group Questions for Chapter 3

- How would you convince your peers that graphic novels have a place in the English/language arts curriculum?
- In your present teaching context, do you think graphic novels would better be used as supplemental or primary texts?
- What literary devices do you regularly teach that would lend themselves to using graphic novels?
- How could you use graphic novels in the critical analysis of literature?
- As ELA teachers, how can you reassure parents that the content of graphic novels is appropriate for their children?

CHAPTER FOUR

Using Graphic Novels to Teach History

ANTICIPATION GUIDE

Directions: Read each statement carefully and decide whether you agree or disagree with it, placing a check mark in the appropriate Before Reading column. When you have finished reading and studying Chapter 4, return to the guide and decide whether your anticipations need to be changed by placing a check mark in the appropriate After Reading column.

	BEFORE READING		AFTER READING	
	Agree	*Disagree*	*Agree*	*Disagree*
1. Most history instruction in today's schools focuses too much on facts and not enough on understanding historical events.				
2. History instruction should always include multiple texts.				
3. Narrative texts describing historical events are a good supplement to textbooks.				
4. Graphic novels can make complex texts easier to read and more interesting for students.				
5. Using multiple texts at varying levels is good instruction but difficult to implement in practice.				

These panels from *Trinity: A Graphic History of the First Atomic Bomb* (Fetter-Vorm, 2013) illustrate the power of graphic art to bring history to life. With a few well-selected words and compelling artwork, the author brings home the uncertainty and fear that accompanied the first detonation. Note the matter-of-fact dialogue and black-and-white graphics.

> To look at graphic literature as a product of its time and place is
> to catch a glimpse of the political and cultural zeitgeist of a nation.
>
> —Michael Cromer and Penny Clark, *Getting Graphic with the Past:*
> *Graphic Novels and the Teaching of History*

TRADITIONALLY, STUDENTS' DEVELOPMENT of historical, social, and political understanding relied heavily on the textbook (e.g., Goodlad, 1984; VanSledright & Kelly, 1998), with teacher instruction focused on the factual information presented in the text. Throughout the years, textbooks have been criticized (e.g., Beck & McKeown, 1991; McCabe, 1993; VanSledright & Kelly, 1998; Wineburg, 2001) because of their use of the omniscient and invisible narrator. This mundane style of writing leads to a decontextualized, confusing text perceived by most students as beyond question (Beck, McKeown, & Worthy, 1995). These emphases have limited students, and adult members of society as well, to a narrow view of historical events and their implications for current cultural and political issues.

Historians know that there is no one big truth but rather multiple interpretations of historical events and even more explanations of why the events took place, what they might mean, and how they might provide insight into current events. Hence, any serious study of history and the other social sciences must always carefully consider multiple texts. In this chapter, we will focus on instruction and learning in history, but the principles we propose apply to all of the social sciences.

Recently, history educators as well as literacy researchers (e.g., Nokes, 2010; Nokes, Dole, & Hacker, 2007; Shanahan & Shanahan, 2008; Wineburg, 1991, 1998, 2001) have called for a different approach to instruction. These educators advocate classroom instruction in which students not only learn about the past but also learn how to study the past. They argue, and we agree with some caution (Brozo, Moorman, Meyer, & Stewart, 2013), that middle and secondary teachers need to foster critical literacy and thinking in our students that reflects the way historians engage in their discipline. This approach to instruction requires the reading of multiple sources to develop an understanding of the past. Using this conceptualization of history instruction as a framework, VanSledright and Kelly (1998) identify four reading practices that they believe are essential to historical learning: (1) recognizing that historical texts are representations of the past constructed by authors who have biases, (2) building event models from multiple recounts of the past to analyze historical evidence, (3) sourcing texts and their perspectives in relation to other sources and the historical context, and (4) reading to ascertain the author's purpose and bias. Many in education believe that teachers can use graphic novels and comics to scaffold students' abilities to read critically and think historically while motivating and engaging the students in the process. For example, Boerman-Cornell (2010) argues:

and require careful planning and explicit teaching. True classroom dialogues, and therefore Socratic Seminars, will more resemble adult conversations where all speakers have equal standing. Tommy believes that using Socratic Seminars challenges students to think deeply and critically about the Spartan culture and the similarities and differences with our own culture. Each day after reading one chapter from the book, Tommy plans to engage his students in a seminar.

Tommy's first order of business is the same as for any instructional event. He must make sure he has the background knowledge necessary to carry out the lesson. With Socratic Seminars, it is even more important to have a broad background because at their best, the seminars are unpredictable and require knowledge beyond the basics. Tommy reviews the historical background of Ancient Greece, particularly of Socrates and Sparta. He carefully reads all of *300* and rereads the first chapter several times, at least once out loud. He needs to continue this background preparation until he is very comfortable that he has a high level of knowledge on the topic.

For the last step in preparation, Tommy creates multiple discussion questions. Remembering that the narrative is carried by both text and pictures, Tommy develops questions that address both. Foremost in his mind is not to create questions that have simple or right/wrong answers, but rather to create questions that challenge the students to be thoughtful and critical. Here is a list of questions that were generated:

1. The title of this chapter is "Honor." How would you describe the Spartans' code of honor? How is it different from YOUR code of honor?
2. Look carefully at the pictures that show the punishment of Stelios. What emotions do these pictures evoke?
3. What do you think the author is trying to say with the telling of the story of Leonidas as a boy and his slaying of the wolf? What does this say about the Spartans? What is it about the story that is so celebrated by the soldiers?
4. Why does the illustrator color the wolf black?
5. Look carefully at the pictures and read carefully the text on the page that shows the men sleeping but the king awake. What do you think this page is telling you about what to expect in the rest of the story?
6. Carefully examine the picture that shows a close-up of the face of the Persian ambassador bringing a message from King Xerxes. How does this picture portray the ambassador?
7. On this page, the illustrator shows the procession of the Persian ambassador and Leonidas from above. Why does he choose this perspective?
8. What does *300* reveal about the Spartan way of life?

When introducing *300* and Socratic Seminars, Tommy shares his expectations with students and clarifies his role. He advises students to focus on the meaning of both the printed text and the graphic techniques. He then informs students that they will be discussing the graphic novel in Socratic Seminars, and that the goal of the seminar is for students to assume as much responsibility as possible for their learning. Knowing the importance of clear and explicit expectations, he shares a "ground rules" handout that clearly lays out student behavioral expectations. He downloads the handout shown in Figure 4.1 from the Socrates Seminar International website (www.socraticseminars.com) and distributes it to the class. Each of the rules is clearly explained. Tommy assures the students that he will refocus the class when the guidelines are not being followed.

On the first day, Tommy reads aloud chapter 1. He pauses periodically to share various graphic techniques that enhance the story. After reading, he revisits the concept of Socratic Seminar and what his expectations for the students are. He begins with a brief historical lesson on Socrates, noting that the famous philosopher and the Spartans in *300* shared a time and place.

Next Tommy begins with the questions. He starts with the first question: The title of this chapter is "Honor." How would you describe the Spartans' code of honor? How is it different from YOUR code of honor? At first students are slow to respond. However, Tommy provides adequate wait time, refusing to fall into a student-teacher-student-teacher response pattern. After a few moments, one of the more outgoing students responds. Lily thinks the Spartan code of honor is very different from hers. She shares that she would not want to live in a world with such harsh expectations. Lily believes that honor is looking for a peaceful solution. Now the discussion becomes lively, with many students sharing their view of

Figure 4.1. Socratic Seminar Ground Rules

1. Speak so that all can hear you.

2. Listen closely.

3. Speak without raising hands.

4. Refer to the text.

5. Talk to each other, not just to the leader.

6. Ask for clarification. Don't stay confused.

7. Invite and allow others to speak.

8. Consider all viewpoints and ideas.

9. Know that you are responsible for the quality of the seminar.

honor and how it compares to the Spartan way. Tommy allows students to share their views, but directs the discussion through follow-up questions. Throughout the discussion, he encourages quiet students to share their thoughts.

Tommy asks for a volunteer to answer the final question: What does *300* reveal about the Spartan way of life? He is pleased when Matt, one of his best students, raises his hand. Matt's response is that the Spartans were tough and mean. Tommy asks Matt to move to the smart board and show how both the text and the graphics support his answer. Matt manipulates the text on the smart board to the sixth and seventh pages. Matt explains how the pictures show how a young soldier who is exhausted is beaten almost to death in front of the Spartan warriors. He reads the text starting on the bottom of page 6: "Stelios. You clown." "Yes, sir." "I'm ready to take my punishment, sir." "Whukk." "Krak." "Whukk." "We wonder if Stelios will die." "Only one among us can stop this." "Only HE." "Enough." "But the captain does not hear." "HE does not repeat the order." Matt explains how the pictures illustrate the cruelty of the beating, but also how the Spartans viewed it as necessary to create toughness and discipline among the soldiers. Tommy is pleased: Matt's answer not only reveals a deep understanding of the story but also educates the rest of the class in how to process graphic novel text. To conclude class, Tommy provides an "exit slip" (Fisher, Brozo, Frey, & Ivey, 2011). The role of assessment for this lesson is to determine the effectiveness of both *300* and the Socratic Seminar as well as the level of engagement of students. Tommy needs to know both how well students participated (nearly impossible to do accurately during teaching) and if they learned from the lesson. To do this, Tommy has created an exit slip (see Figure 4.2). The students complete this before they leave class.

Figure 4.2. Exit Slip for Socratic Seminar

Using a scale of from 1 (strongly disagree) to 5 (strongly agree), describe your participation in today's Socratic Seminar:

I actively participated in the seminar.	1	2	3	4	5
I used *300* to support my responses.	1	2	3	4	5
I referred to graphic techniques to support my responses.	1	2	3	4	5
I learned from what others said.	1	2	3	4	5
I developed my own questions pertaining to *300*.	1	2	3	4	5

Write down one or two things you think would improve the seminar.

Write down one or two important things you learned from *300*.

Over the next 4 days, Tommy continues reading *300* and conducting Socratic Seminars. His preparation for each day is less involved than the 1st day, since he no longer needs to do the background preparation. Most of his work is centered on producing quality questions that promote students' interaction with *300*. Learning from each day, he tries to implement strategies to bring out students who are reluctant participators. On the 3rd day, he asks a colleague to observe the lesson, paying special attention to participation patterns and how students refer to *300* to develop questions and answers. This is helpful for the final 2 days.

Over the 5 days, Tommy consciously transitions more and more responsibility to students by encouraging students to ask follow-up questions to elicit additional responses and to compliment classmates. After reading on the 4th day, he places students in five cooperative groups he has carefully selected. Each group is heterogeneous, including students with a range of reading, academic, and social skills. He assigns the groups with the task of writing the seminar questions. He reminds students to make sure the questions directly relate to *300*. He does not give much time, less than 10 minutes, and uses both student-generated and his own questions to conduct the seminar. This procedure is continued on Day Five. However, on the 5th day, Tommy asks students to think of *300* as a whole and create questions that explicitly explore the similarities and differences between Ancient Sparta and the modern United States. For this final seminar, Tommy solely relies on student-generated questions. Some student-generated questions include

- At the end of chapter 1, King Leonidas kills the Persian messenger. What do the pictures on the final page of the chapter say about this action? What do you think about the killing of the messenger?
- In chapter 2, Leonidas's wife says, "Spartan, come back with your shield—or on it." What does she mean? What does this say about the Spartans?
- Chapter 3 describes the overwhelming force the Persians bring against the 300 Spartan soldiers. What do you think was going through the minds of the Spartans as they looked out on the Persian army? How would you feel if you were one of the Spartans?
- After the initial battle described at the beginning of chapter 4, Xerxes, the Persian king, meets with Leonidas. Describe the meeting. What does Leonidas's response to Xerxes tell you about the Greeks and the Spartans? Would you describe the response as heroic or foolish or a combination of both?
- In chapter 5, all 300 of the Spartans are killed. Why is the chapter titled "Victory"?

Tommy believes that the student-created questions demonstrate that students have learned about Sparta through reading *300* and participating in Socratic Seminars. He believes that his students have a better understanding of the Spartan way of life and Greek culture than in past years.

UNDERSTANDING NATIONAL POLICY USING THE *9/11 REPORT: A GRAPHIC ADAPTATION*

Kathy teaches an advanced course in American government. Always searching for innovative ways to scaffold her students' learning, Kathy decides to explore graphic novels appropriate for her course and students. Familiar with both Kathy's teaching philosophy and her expectations for her students, we suggest Kathy read *The 9/11 Report: A Graphic Adaptation* (2006). We believe that Sid Jacobson and Ernie Colón's graphic novel, based on the *Final Report of the National Commission on Terrorist Attacks upon the United States* (National Commission on Terrorist Attacks, 2004) provides Kathy with a unique teaching tool through which she can provide her students insight into not only structure of national security leading up to the 9/11 attacks but into the political aftermath as well.

The 9/11 Report: A Graphic Adaptation is a complex and mature piece of literature that Kathy deems appropriate for her college-bound seniors. For Kathy's students, who were young children on the day of the attacks, this may well be their first scholarly interaction with the events of the day. While the graphic novel does not candy-coat the tragedy of the attacks, it provides a medium through which high school students can engage and access the text in a meaningful way.

Kathy believes the authors' choice to immediately jump into the horrific events onboard Flights 11, 175, 77, and 93 will capture her students' attention and motivate them to read further to investigate the causes of the tragedy. The remainder of the book provides the information her bright and inquisitive students will want to know. Chapters 2–8 cover decades of history highlighting the rise of Osama Bin Laden and al-Qaeda, and the United States' inability to initially fathom and later predict and respond to jihadist terrorism on U.S. soil. Chapters 9 and 10 return to the September 11 attacks, cataloging the actions of the heroes of 9/11 and the United States' military response. Finally, chapters 11–13 discuss the lessons of 9/11 and how to move forward and improve national security in the wake of such an unthinkable tragedy. While Kathy believes her students will be motivated to learn about the topic, she does not believe her students have the stamina to read the official government document. She recognizes the scaffolds the graphic adaption provides her students. She appreciates the authors' ability to identify and include essential information and the illustrator's ability to provide additional but critical information through the artwork. All in all, Kathy believes this is an excellent choice for her students. However, she recognizes the need to inform parents of the controversial nature of the book. Prior to beginning the unit, Kathy sends home a letter detailing why she is using the book and the academic value of the unit. She also holds a class meeting, during which she shares with her students the need for maturity that reading such a sensitive book entails.

Because of the mature topic and complex graphic format of *9/11*, Kathy plans to read the first chapter aloud to the class. She also decides that two-column notes (Donohoo, 2010) would be an excellent strategy to guide students through the reading. Kathy decides to "think aloud" her thought process as she engages with the text and models how to complete the two-column notes. This will allow her to demonstrate how she reads the text, how she makes sense of the difficult topic, and how she utilizes the two-column notes to process both the text and the pictures. After the first chapter, the class will be expected to read the graphic novel over a 6-day period. Students will be required to read two chapters per day and respond to the text with the two-column notes. Kathy also plans to begin each class period with a discussion about the previous day's reading and believes the two-column notes will provide a springboard for discussion.

As with the Socratic Seminars, two-column notes provide an excellent opportunity to help students become more self-directed while engaging them in deeper processing of text. Over the 6 days of reading the book, students will be expected to take increasing responsibility for constructing and completing two-column notes. This strategy has been shown to be a highly effective learning and study strategy (Donohoo, 2010; Fisher & Frey, 2008).

Implementing two-column notes is a simple process. The essential component of the strategy is a worksheet in the form of a two-column T. The left column is smaller, usually about one-third of the page. Key concepts, vocabulary, or main ideas are written in this column. In the right column, explanations or elaborations of the ideas are written out. Initially, teachers need to decide how much assistance to provide for students. In a typical first example on the next page (Figure 4.3), Kathy's students have been provided with five key concepts in the left column, and one written-out elaboration in the right column. Over the next six instructional sessions, students will be expected to provide more of the key concepts and all of the elaborations. The ultimate goal with two-column notes is for students to independently decide to use two-column notes during their reading, or lectures or video presentations. The two-column notes form is easily made by either folding a piece of paper or drawing the lines in the one-third to two-thirds dimensions. (Side note: The authors often use two-column notes in their own studying and reading).

For the first lesson, Kathy introduces her students to the two-column notes organizer she has created. She explains the ultimate goal of independence and describes how two-column notes will be used as they read the graphic novel.

Figure 4.3. Chapter One Two-Column Notes

Key Concepts	Explanations (be sure to comment on graphics as appropriate)
1. The hijacking (pp. 3–17)	1. The timeline of events for each of the four hijacked planes reveals how well prepared the hijackers were, and how ill prepared airport security was, as well as that a lack of communication between the planes and air traffic control were evident. Graphics demonstrate the brutality of the hijackers as well as the violence and devastating impact of the planes on the World Trade Center. The pictures of the explosions of the World Trade Center are particularly powerful. The pictures of the violent struggles onboard the planes bring out a sense of desperation.
2. Heroes on Flight 93 (pp. 11–17)	2.
3. Lack of preparedness for the terrorist attack (pp. 16–25)	3.
4. Chaos at the White House (pp. 26–28)	4.
5. The 9/11 Commission's conclusions (p. 29)	5.

Students are provided with the two-column notes form below, and Kathy projects a digital copy on the smart board she completes as she reads (Figure 4.3)

Kathy reads aloud the first 17 pages of the novel. She is enthusiastic and animated in her reading. She encourages students to ask questions, and pauses often to think aloud about how she is making sense of both the text and the graphics. When she is done with the first section, she explains how and why she wrote the text in the right column for the first key concept. She asks students if they have anything to add or if they have questions about what she wrote. She then proceeds to read the next four sections of the chapter, periodically stopping to add to the two-column notes worksheet. While discussing the five key concepts, she and the students coauthor the explanations.

When she finishes, she assigns chapters 2 and 3, providing students with a second two-column notes guide. On this one, she provides the students with five key concepts in the left column but nothing in the right column. Having carefully planned her time, she gives students the last part of the class period to begin reading and filling in the worksheet. As students read, she circulates among the students to answer questions and provide assistance to any students who are struggling.

At the beginning of the next class, Kathy provides students with a few minutes to meet with a partner to share and discuss their two-column notes. She then engages the students in a whole-class discussion about the chapter, focusing first on the key concepts from the two-column notes guide. As the discussion progresses, she encourages the students to take more responsibility for its direction. When she finishes, she assigns the next two chapters and provides the students with the next two-column notes guide. With this guide, she provides three key concepts and leaves three spaces blank, instructing students to fill in two additional concepts as well as the elaborations. Again, time is left at the end for students to begin reading.

This basic pattern (review and read, discuss the chapters, assign the next chapter, begin reading) is followed for the next 5 days. Progressively, each two-column notes guide provides students with fewer key concepts until the final guide is an empty two-column notes form. In addition, after the 5th day, the opening discussions are done in small groups with Kathy circulating among the groups. The key to Kathy's instruction with this book is her expectation that students assume more and more responsibility for both the discussions and the two-column notes, and she provides explicit instructions on how they can do this. Throughout, she encourages students to process both the written text and the graphics to process and comprehend the narrative.

As a culminating activity, Kathy instructs her students to use the information collected through their two-column notes to write a two-page summary of their understanding of *The 9/11 Report*. She emphasizes that their writing should be in a form the general public can understand and should address both the written text and the artwork from the book. The summaries clearly demonstrate that the graphic adaptation of the report made a difficult text accessible and interesting to the students.

EXPLORING WORLD WAR II
THROUGH GRAPHIC NOVEL BOOK CLUBS

Jenny is a middle-grades history teacher who teaches a heterogeneously grouped world history class. Her typical class includes students who read above, at, and below grade level. In addition, her class also includes students identified as special-needs learners, including English language learners. Frustrated with her inability to identify appropriate reading materials to engage her students in meaningful literacy tasks, Jenny recently decided to pursue a graduate degree in literacy. After participating in a young adult literature course, Jenny decided to incorporate graphic novels into her 8th-grade history class. Jenny believes that having students read graphic novels and participate in book clubs will provide background necessary for understanding the events and consequences of World War II. Because her class is heterogeneously grouped, Jenny decides to identify five graphic novels whose topics and reading levels vary: *Trinity, A Graphic History of the First Atomic Bomb* (Fetter-Vorm, 2012), *Anne Frank: The Anne Frank House Authorized Graphic Biography* (Jacobson & Colón, 2010), *Resistance, Book 1* (Jablonski & Purvis, 2010), *Island of Terror: Battle of Iwo Jima* (Hama & Williams, 2006b), and *The Tide Turns: D-Day Invasion* (Murray & Williams, 2007).

Not only is Jenny excited about incorporating varying levels of texts, she recognizes the power of book clubs in a middle-grades classroom. Middle-grade educators have long promoted the important the role of book clubs and literature circles in middle-grade classrooms (e.g., Daniels, 2002; Hill, Noe, & King, 2003). According to Latendresse (2004), book clubs suit middle-grade students because young adolescents benefit from working in small collaborative groups through which they can develop a joint understanding of text. Book clubs and literature circles provide scaffolds to students who may not read as quickly and proficiently as their peers. When given an opportunity to participate in book clubs, "struggling" readers are given a voice and will participate in literacy tasks from which they may otherwise disengage (Blum, Lipsett, & Yocom, 2002).

Jenny's school recently purchased a laptop for each child, and her students are motivated to use the technology. To take advantage of both the graphic novels and technology, she decides to introduce electronic book clubs, hoping they will motivate her students to learn more deeply about the topic and engage in discussion that will foster a richer understanding of different facets of the war. Electronic book clubs provide students with an opportunity to combine traditional literacies (i.e., reading a novel) with new literacies (discussing books online). The integration of electronic book clubs supports the National Education Technology Plan (2010), which calls for the use of technology in content learning. Jenny sees the electronic book clubs as a win-win situation in which she engages students in rich content learning while incorporating 21st-century skills.

Initiating the Book Clubs. Jenny begins the online book clubs with 2 days of preparation. First, Jenny introduces her students to the format she plans to incorporate for the online discussion. She decides to use a Moodle (www. moodle.org) platform because students can use both a synchronistic chat tool as well as communicate through asynchronistic threads. During class, students are given an opportunity to respond to a post made earlier by Jenny welcoming them to their book club as well a chat with members of the class. Students quickly adapt to the Moodle platform, replying not only to Jenny's post but chatting with classmates as well. Next, Jenny delivers book talks about the graphic novels she selected.

Book Talk One: *Trinity, A Graphic History of the First Atomic Bomb.* The most challenging of the book choices, this historical narrative by Jonathon Fetter-Vorm, published in 2012, vividly captures the drama of the race to develop the first atomic bomb. Fetter-Vorm clearly depicts the progress of nuclear understanding from the laboratories of 19th-century Europe to the massive war effort of the secret Manhattan project and finally to the horrors of Nagasaki and Hiroshima. *Trinity* not only delves into the historical account of the development of the atomic bomb, it shares the sciences behind the behind the bomb as well as the moral implications with which all associated with the development and decision to use the bomb had to wrestle.

Jenny shares with her students that *Trinity* is a very technical graphic novel. Along with the history of the atomic bomb, Fetter-Vorm provides the reader with the science behind the atomic bomb. Jenny discusses how the artwork and author make you feel like you are part of the secret mission and that you, too, can help in the discoveries. She encourages her students interested in science to select this book.

Book Talk Two: *Anne Frank: The Anne Frank House Authorized Graphic Biography.* While not as demanding as *Trinity, Anne Frank* is a challenging and complex graphic novel. This is another outstanding graphic novel by the team of Sid Jacobson and Ernie Colón. The result of 2 years of extensive research at the Anne Frank House in Amsterdam, it was published in 2010. The book begins with the lives of Anne's parents, Otto and Edith Frank, a well-to-do Jewish couple living in Frankfurt, Germany, in the early 20th century. It follows their life through World War I to their marriage in 1925, Anne's birth in 1929, and the rise of Nazism in Germany. It continues with the Franks' move to Amsterdam and their years of hiding in a secret annex to escape the Nazi occupation of the Netherlands. It finally depicts their betrayal and deportation to the death camps and Anne's tragic death, leading to Otto's work to get Anne's diary published. In addition to the narrative, the book provides brief historical perspectives on the events leading up to World War II, Nazi Germany, and the "Final Solution," Hitler's plan to annihilate Europe's Jewish population.

In her book talk, Jenny emphasizes the extraordinary power that the graphics bring to the narrative of Anne's life and provides an outline of the narrative. Next, to reinforce the relationship between the book and the digital emphasis of the lesson, she takes the class to the publisher's website (www.us.macmillan.com/annefrank-2/SidJacobson), where she plays two videos, an animated short of a passage from the book, and an interview with the authors and the director of the Anne Frank House. Finally, she takes the class on a tour of the official Anne Frank House Museum website (www.annefrank.org/). She encourages students with an interest in the Holocaust to choose this book club.

Book Talk Three: *Resistance, Book 1*. This novel, the least challenging of all the book club choices, written by Carla Jablonski and illustrated by Leland Purvis, with color by Hilary Sycamore, tells the story of two young adolescents as they navigate life during World War II. Paul and Marie live in a French "free zone," a village the Germans do not occupy. However, the children's lives do not remain unscathed. Their father is taken as a prisoner of war by the German army, and whispers of horrors reach their village. These horrors become personal when the parents of a Jewish friend, Henri, disappear. Marie and Paul take it upon themselves to hide and protect their friend from the Nazis. However, their secret is discovered and they find themselves part of the French Resistance. *Resistance* is an excellent choice for students who may not be ready for the demands of *Anne Frank* but want to learn more about the Holocaust and those who took a stand against it.

During the book talk, Jenny highlights the important role Marie, Paul, and Henri play in the Resistance by sharing several incidents from the story. For example, when Marie and Paul sneak Henri out of their village into the occupied zone in search of his parents, the children face dangers and even witness a member of the Resistance being shot. She discusses how the picture and colors used help to tell the story of Marie, Paul, and Henri and encourages students who would like to know about the Resistance to read the book.

Book Talk Four: *Island of Terror: Battle of Iwo Jima* (Graphic History). A simpler read than *Trinity* and *Anne Frank*, this historical narrative is written by Larry Hama and illustrated by Anthony Williams with cover art by Gary Erskine. The novel includes well-written historical accounts of the Battle of Iwo Jima at both the beginning and end of the graphic novel. The information provided at the beginning of the novel depicts events leading to the Battle of Iwo Jima, while the information at the end informs the reader of events after the battle. The graphic novel details the enormous strategic importance of this tiny island in the South Pacific, and how its capture by American forces hastened the end of the war with Japan. For 36 days in early 1945, 70,000 U.S. troops, mostly marines, fought a bloody battle against 23,000 Japanese troops dug into bunkers, tunnels, and pillboxes on the island. In the end, over 20,000 Japanese died, refusing to surrender despite the impossibility of victory. Seven thousand Americans also died.

In her book talk, Jenny begins with the historical context for the book. She outlines the World War II battle of the Pacific, beginning with the events leading up to the bombing of Pearl Harbor on December 7, 1941, and continuing through the vicious naval battles and invasions of Pacific islands. She addresses the importance of Iwo Jima as long-range B-29 bombers began to bomb Japan, and how the island provided airfields for saving downed bomber pilots and a base for fighter planes that provided cover for the B-29s. She then previews the graphic novel, paying special attention to the heroes; 27 Congressional Medals of Honor were awarded. She talks about hero Ira Hayes and shows an online version of the most reproduced photo in history, of the raising of the American flag on Mount Surabachi (www.iwojima.com/raising/raisingb.htm). She also points out the valor and courage of the Japanese soldiers who chose to fight to the death. She encourages students with special interests in military tactics and World War II battles to choose this book for their book club.

Book Talk Five: *The Tide Turns: D-Day Invasion* (Graphic History). A sister text to *Island of Terror: Battle of Iwo Jima,* this graphic novel by Doug Murray with art by Anthony Williams and cover art by Richard Elson details the events of the D Day invasion. *The Tide Turns* also includes a historical narrative at the beginning and end of the text, which scaffolds understanding of the graphic novel. Through this engaging narrative, the novel dramatically brings to life the events of the D-Day landings. The story begins as an army of over 150,000 Allied soldiers prepares to invade the beaches of France. Supported by more than 13,000 aircraft, soldiers from the United States, Canada, and Great Britain valiantly battled the Germans in an operation that paved the way for the freedom of Nazi-occupied Europe and the end of Hitler's terrifying regime.

In her book talk, Jenny begins with the historical context for the book. She outlines the World War II European Theater, beginning with the events leading up to the Nazi invasion of Poland and the United States joining the war. She explains the tense relationship that the United States and Great Britain had with the Soviet Union. She then shares a video found on the National D-Day Memorial website (www.dday.org/). After sharing the D-Day overview, she details the importance of the invasion and the fact that within 10 months of the invasion, the Nazi regime had fallen.

After the book talks, Jenny allows her students time to browse through the books. She directs students to write down their three favorites on a "secret ballot." During her planning, she assigns students to book clubs. She makes a special effort to place all students in one of their top choices; however, she uses a combination of students' reading ability and their choices to form reading groups. The next day Jenny announces the book clubs and distributes the books and calendars. Students excitedly peruse the books, and Jenny needs to refocus the class. She informs the groups that they will have 1 week to read their book and provides a calculator to help students determine how many pages their group will need to read each day to finish their reading on time. Jenny informs students that she will provide 20 minutes of class time each day for sustained silent reading. Students will then have the opportunity to discuss the book on-line. Students will be responsible each evening for finishing assigned reading and participating in the book club.

Jenny provides the students with 20 minutes to read. She circulates through the class, monitoring students and providing assistance when needed. A few students have questions about the graphic format, so Jenny provides individual instruction to these students. Fifteen minutes pass, and she gives students a 5-minute warning. After reading, students log on to their Moodle accounts and begin chatting with their peers about the assigned reading. Jenny provides students with the remaining 10 minutes of class to participate in the online discussion. As the class closes, Jenny reminds the students to finish any assigned reading for homework and invites them to continue their discussion using the forum option on Moodle. After school, Jenny visits each group's discussion thread and is pleased to see the amount of "chatter" that has occurred. The discussions indicate that the students enjoy the graphic format. However, Jenny notes some misconceptions in the responses that she addresses during the next class.

This basic pattern (read, then real-time and forum discussions) is followed for the next 4 days. At the end of the 5th day, Jenny places the students in their book clubs. Jenny instructs each group to assume the role of a war correspondent for the national radio news. Working collaboratively, each group is to compose a script for a special feature about their book's events. They have the remainder of the 5th day as well as the 6th to carefully construct the script and then practice reading it. Students are reminded to integrate what they have learned through the online discussion into their scripts.

On the 7th and final day, the students perform their scripts for the class. After each group presents their script, Jenny holds a class debriefing, providing students with opportunities to discuss the unit. Jenny uses the debriefings to fill in important information about events in World War II. Through the discussion it becomes evident to Jenny that the graphic novels have motivated the students to learn more about the war. She feels comfortable that it is time to move into a more comprehensive and focused study of the war.

LOOKING BACK AND MOVING FORWARD

In this chapter, we explored the potential of integrating graphic novels into the history classroom. We shared three approaches used by history teachers in middle and high schools to successfully integrate graphic novels into their instruction. The first approach paired a graphic novel read-aloud with Socratic Seminar to build a joint understanding of an ancient culture that has had a lasting impact on our society. The second approach used the two-column-notes strategy to scaffold a deep understanding of a complex graphic novel read individually by students. Finally, we demonstrated how teachers can manage multiple graphic novels using digital book clubs. In each scenario our teachers creatively employed graphic novels to promote a rich learning environment that motivated and engaged their students.

In the next chapter, you will encounter science teachers who, like the history teachers in this chapter, recognize the exciting possibilities that graphic novels bring to their discipline and their potential to scaffold student learning.

Study Group Questions for Chapter 4

- What do you see as the obstacles in your department to integrating graphic novels into your social studies classrooms? How can these be overcome?

- In your present teaching context, do you think graphic novels would better be used as supplemental or primary texts?

- Identify a lesson or unit that is regularly taught in your department. How could graphic novels be included in the instruction?

- What steps can be taken to convince administrators that graphic novels can make valuable contributions to social studies instruction?

- What role can graphic novels play in differentiating social studies instruction?

CHAPTER FIVE

Using Graphic Novels to Teach Science

ANTICIPATION GUIDE

Directions: Read each statement carefully and decide whether you agree or disagree with it, placing a check mark in the appropriate Before Reading column. When you have finished reading and studying Chapter 5, return to the guide and decide whether your anticipations need to be changed by placing a check mark in the appropriate After Reading column.

	BEFORE READING		AFTER READING	
	Agree	*Disagree*	*Agree*	*Disagree*
1. Graphic novels may be the solution to America's crisis in science education.				
2. Given their multimodal nature, graphic novels are ideal for developing scientific literacy.				
3. Science teachers need to use multiple graphic novels to have an impact on student learning.				
4. Science-related graphic novels and science textbooks are compatible instructional resources.				
5. Science-related graphic novels can teach students science without the need for a teacher.				

In these panels from *The Manga Guide to Relativity* (Yamamoto, Takatsu, & Nitta, 2011), important foundational information about theories of relativity are presented in ways that make this content interesting and understandable to all students, especially those who are struggling and disengaged.

I've seen it numerous times at comic book conventions. If the story is entertaining, kids remember the science because it is presented in context.

—Jay Hosler, *Comic Book Science*

I N HIS AMUSING AND COMPELLING ARGUMENT for the use of comics in the teaching of science, rendered in comic book panels, Jay Hosler (2007), writer, illustrator and biology professor, says through one of his comic characters, "With their unique synthesis of words and art, comics express thoughts and ideas in ways other mediums cannot. In fact, I would argue that comics have been essential to our understanding of the natural world" (p. 4). Hosler's character goes on to urge teachers to use "comics as an intermediary for new, sometimes challenging, ideas from the natural sciences" (p. 7).

Exhortations from Hosler's comic persona aside, numerous benefits for science learning and literacy from graphic novels and comics can be found. From the more effusive supporters of these media, who go so far as to assert that the solution to America's crisis in science education may be more comic books, to those who advocate specific animations, texts, and practices, the voices and evidence for integrating graphic novels and comics into the science classroom are growing. The documented benefits of employing these media in science include (1) gaining student attention and stimulating critical thinking (Cheesman, 2006); (2) fostering greater science learning for all students, particularly reluctant learners (Özdemir, 2010); (3) increasing higher-order achievement (Ausman, Lin, Kidwai, Munyofu, Swain, & Dwyer, 2004); (4) offering easier access to and understanding of science concepts (Witkowski, 1997); (5) clarifying misconceptions (Kabapınar, 2005); (6) making science learning fun (Olson, 2008); and (7) creating unique options for assessing students' science knowledge (Song, Heo, Krumenaker, & Tippins, 2008).

Science-related graphic novels and comics, with their blend of dialogue and images, allow students to gain and interpret science concepts and information through a unique and accessible format, opening a window to science for even the most reluctant learners. These multimodal resources can be powerful teaching and learning tools in science, as Knain (2006) underscores:

> Multimodality should be . . . an aspect of the competence of science literacy that students are expected to acquire, but also as a valuable tool for developing science literacy, by enabling transformations across different modes of representation and different contextual presuppositions, in particular, between everyday and scientific contextual frames. (p. 659)

More than either visual art or literature alone, today's graphic novels and comics have evolved into an engaging tool for transmitting information and stimulating critical thinking in this multimedia world (Kerr & Culhane, 2000). The multimodal nature of graphic novels would seem, then, to make them ideal resources for supporting adolescents' learning of science and promoting scientific literacy.

Shanahan and Shanahan (2008, 2012) argue that for students to be judged scientifically literate, they must be proficient in the discourses of science, which include reading, writing, and talking science. According to Carrier (2005), scientifically literate students not only have the facility to read scientific texts with understanding, but also can describe natural phenomena and predict outcomes, and demonstrate curiosity about everyday experience by asking and seeking answers to their own questions. Similarly, Hand, Prain, and Yore (2001), along with Norris and Phillips (2003), describe the truly science-literate student as someone who possesses proficiency in science language and thinking and is also able to make informed judgments on scientific societal issues.

These characteristics of a scientifically literate student can be nurtured by graphic novels and comics, as the typical science textbook may be uninspiring (Rowe, 2005) and difficult to access, especially for struggling readers and learners of English (Fang, 2006; Monnin, 2010; Webb, 2009). Unlike textbooks, graphic novels are from youths' popular culture, which is integral to their lives, so it can help bridge the gap between inside- and outside-of-school literacies (Morrison, Bryan, & Chilcoat, 2002). Furthermore, graphic novelists and comic book writers present content in a manner that can be used to encourage students to become critical consumers of science, a core goal of science literacy (Hapgood & Palincsar, 2007).

As the influence of the Common Core State Standards expands, there is a growing recognition of the central role of literacy and language in the learning of science (Norris & Phillips, 2003; Pearson, Moje, & Greenleaf, 2010; Yore & Treagust, 2006). Nonetheless, developing proficiency in the language of science for struggling and second language learners will present ever-increasing challenges for secondary science and literacy teachers (Carrier, 2005; Faggella-Luby, Graner, Deschler, & Drew, 2012). In the remainder of this chapter, we describe several ways that science teachers have used graphic novels to engage and ensure access to essential content for all their students.

INSTRUCTIONAL PRACTICES
WITH GRAPHIC NOVELS IN SCIENCE

Genome: A Read-Aloud for Biology

Imagine a menacing future world in which the entire human genetic code or genome is patented by a single megacorporation and all human reproduction is strictly controlled. Parents must apply for licenses to have children and must make mortgage payments to keep them. This is the dark premise for the graphic novel *Genome* by Andrew Glasgow and JM Schichtel (n.d.) and how it is introduced by Jared to his high school biology students at the outset of a new unit on DNA and genetics. Jared decides to use this gripping read-aloud as accompaniment and counterpoint to the chapter on the topic in the course textbook. He reasons that his general education students will find the facts and information about genes and human genetics more interesting and their learning will be more long lasting if he links the topic to a compelling graphic narrative.

Every class session, 2 to 3 days per week depending on the block schedule, Jared reads aloud from *Genome* directly after a short midclass break. Although he asks his students first and foremost to enjoy the story and the visual information, which he shares on the document camera, he also requests that they respond to focused listening prompts designed to foster critical thinking about human genetics and relate the graphic novel content to what is being read and studied in the class textbook.

For example, when reading from the part in *Genome* where Glasgow references actual legal precedent for corporate ownership of genetic code, Jared makes the issue more "real" for his students by also distributing to the class an Op-Ed piece from the *Washington Post* titled "Who Owns Your DNA? Not Who You Think" (Rosenfeld & Mason, 2013). The authors present facts about how large corporations own patents giving them the exclusive right to examine certain human DNA, making it impossible for doctors, except for those willing to accept the legal risks, to test related genes of patients for potentially life-threatening mutations. The Supreme Court will be hearing arguments and the authors urge it to rectify this situation. With his students' interest piqued, Jared asks them to conduct Internet research on related laws that exist in their state. He also asks them to use facts from the textbook chapter to write a letter to one of their members of the House of Representatives taking a stand on whether corporations should be allowed to own human genome patents.

Jared has little trouble gaining and holding his students' attention during his read-aloud of *Genome*. Students are drawn into the story through the author's use of realistic characters, as well as the illustrator's depiction of the range of human emotion experienced by the characters. The story follows Mallow, a single father working in construction after dropping out of college. He struggles to keep his son, Damon, a talented violinist, from the grip of a monolithic corporation that owns Damon's genetic material. In spite of his best efforts, Mallow's son has been foreclosed on and taken away by Genome, the name of the evil corporation that holds mortgages on human genetic material. The plot takes us to a place in the not-so-distant future with fully computerized cars and holographic video games. Our government has become swallowed up in greed, controlled by monolithic industry. Crumbling from immense debt and massive unemployment, America seems doomed. It is up to Mallow to discover how to rescue his son from the grips of this decaying empire and from the custody of Genome Inc.

In spite of its dark themes, *Genome* is a lively read, and because the story is based on a screenplay, the graphic novel has a cinematic feel. Jared takes full advantage of these features by periodically involving students in impromptu reader's theater activities. He makes multiple copies of the relevant pages and invites individuals to participate. For example, during the scene where Genome's thugs come to repossess Mallow's son, Damon, Jared has four eager volunteers join him in the front of the class. After taking assigned roles—two are the Genome heavies, one is Mallow, and one Damon—they quickly read over their lines to prepare. Then, as Jared sets it up and takes the narrator parts, the students reenact this dramatic scene, much to the delight of their classmates.

Afterward, Jared prods students to consider whether this frightening dystopic future can ever become a reality in their lifetimes. Most agree it isn't possible, while some take the position that governments already know about and control people through the Internet, mobile phones, and digital navigation. Jared then refocuses his class on issues related to genetic engineering, particularly on stem cells, the topic they have been covering with their textbook. He forms pairs of students and has them respond to one of the five SPAWN writing prompts. SPAWN is one way to support daily context-focused writing (Brozo & Simpson, 2007; Martin, Martin, & O'Brien, 1984). The SPAWN acronym represents five categories of prompts:

S: *Special Powers*—Students are given the power to change an aspect of the text or topic.

P: *Problem Solving*—Students are asked to write solutions to problems posed or suggested by the books being read or material being studied.

A: *Alternative Viewpoints*—Students write about a topic or story from a unique perspective.

W: *What If?*— Similar to *Special Powers,* the teacher introduces the aspect of the topic or story that has changed, then asks students to write based on that change.

N: *Next*—Students are asked to write in anticipation of what the author will discuss next.

These prompts can be crafted in a limitless variety of ways to stimulate students' meaningful thinking about content area topics (Fisher et al., 2011). The writing prompted by SPAWN is typically short in length and can be kept in students' class notebooks or logs. Jared's SPAWN prompts require his students to write thoughtfully and verifiably about stem cells. Jared designs these prompts in a way that not only requires his students to use textual evidence in their responses, but also instigates critical thinking about differing perspectives on stem cell research, its medical value and ethics, and the role of government.

Special Powers. The president of the United States has assigned you to be chair of the committee on funding stem cell research. He has given you full authority to make decisions regarding the funding of stem cell research. How will you use your power?

Problem Solving. You are the lead researcher in a lab that specializes in stem cell research. Your lab is located in a conservative state. You are offered private funding from a major corporation. What do you do?

Alternative Viewpoints. You are a journalist who has been assigned to report on a university debate on stem cell research. What do you hear?

What If? What if the federal government decided to provide unlimited funding for stem cell research?

Next. Your child has just been in an accident. The doctors say he is paralyzed and will never walk again. However, you have been offered an opportunity have your child participate in an experimental therapy involving embryonic stem cells. What do you do next?

A student pair writing to the *Problem Solving* prompt responds in this way:

> We will accept private funding; however, we will only conduct experimentation with adult stem cells. We refuse to experiment with embryonic stem cells not only because we are located in a conservative state but because of our own personal beliefs. We believe there is no harm done in extracting adult stem cells from already mature living tissues; there's no harm done to the donor of the stem cells; the recipients who receive the products of their own stem cells will not experience immune rejection. Adult stem cells are proved to be highly beneficial and effective in curing disease. We oppose embryonic stem cell research because we do not agree it is ethical to sacrifice a life to help continue another.

A pair of students writing to the *Alternative Viewpoints* prompt composes the following:

> At this debate we heard opinions from people with different views concerning stem cell research. One group, Group A, supported embryonic stem cell research, and the other group, Group B, supported adult stem cell research.

Group A backed up its opinions by stating how versatile embryonic stem cells can be. They have the ability to form all cell types, such as insulin-secreting cells, nerves and heart cells. Also, embryonic stem cells have the ability to repair cells damaged by a heart attack by forming heart cells, as stated above. They also mentioned that although embryonic stem cell research involves the destruction of human life, it has the potential to cure diseases that could continue the life of another.

Group B defended their stance by saying adult stem research involved no ethical issues because no lives are destroyed. There is low risk to tumor growth and these cells will not be rejected by the immune system. Also, they stated that adult stem cells can be used to treat several major diseases, including leukemia, lymphoma, and some inherited blood disorders.

Each group clearly had interesting and valid information to back up their viewpoints in this debate.

These prompts sample students' ability to read texts closely and to make logical inferences from them, as well as to cite specific evidence when writing to support conclusions drawn from the texts. This is a critical Common Core literacy standard, and Jared's students' responses provide evidence of these important reading skills. SPAWN writing challenges the students to combine big, provocative ideas posed in the graphic novel *Genome* about the role of government and private industry in genetic research and patent rights with the specific information on stem cells gleaned from the biology textbook.

By reading aloud from *Genome* during the study of genes and genetics, Jared is able to stimulate interest in the topic, which translates into greater involvement in unit lessons, increased learning of essential information, and interpretive and critical thinking (Albright & Ariail, 2005). Additionally, Jared's adolescent students are the beneficiaries of his fluent and expressive reading (Dreher, 2003), as well as his modeling the important work of navigating uniquely formatted graphic novel text, panels, and gutters (Rosen, 2009).

A final bonus is that once the unit concludes, many of Jared's students are eager to read *Genome* on their own. It delights him to have to set up a checkout system with the graphic novel due to such high interest. Students seeking out and reading on their own books they first encounter through read-alouds has been a well-documented benefit of this practice (Brozo & Tomlinson, 1986; Serafini & Giorgis, 2003)

Going to the Moon with *T-Minus*: Middle-Grades Science

When Melanie receives funding from a foundation in her school district for a grant she wrote to buy class sets of graphic novels to use in science, she is overjoyed. She has never written a grant before and has kept her expectations low, but reacts immediately to the positive news by going online and purchasing 30 copies of *T-Minus: The Race to the Moon* (Ottaviani, Cannon, & Cannon, 2009). She has a personal copy of this graphic novel and is poised to acquire multiple copies to use with her middle-graders for an upcoming unit in their science textbooks on space and its exploration.

T-Minus is a nonfiction, black-and-white graphic novel that gives a historical account of the American-Soviet space race and how competition served to catapult Kennedy's vision of putting a man on the moon within a decade. The novel begins with a conversation between two American scientists talking within NACA, the precursor to NASA, discussing the failed launch of the Russian *Semyorka* rocket. From the scientists' discussion, the reader is gradually introduced to the space race and the premier scientists who were instrumental in the rocket and rocket systems design that helped realize manned space flight. Ottaviani focuses on the men and women who worked to make the space program successful instead of focusing on the astronauts themselves. Careful attention is given to the accomplishments of both the American and the Soviet space programs, from documenting the first successful launch of an orbiting satellite by the Russians to the Americans putting the first man on the moon.

Throughout the book Ottaviani uses a T-Minus timeline as a means of keeping the reader informed of the passage of time between important developments in the space race. Sidebars are also used to highlight successes and failures of both the American and Soviet rocket trials as well as to call attention to vocabulary that is germane to rocket science. Although the story is very dense, packing a great amount of detail into the 124 pages of the novel, the detailed illustrations help scaffold the reader's understanding of the information and ideas. The timeline used throughout the book is helpful in keeping track of the sequence of events. Also, Ottaviani's use of sidebars to document failures and successes of attempted and successful space missions helps keep the progress of space travel in context. For students, there is good contextual use of science vocabulary, such as *pressure, humidity, g-force,* and *satellite.* To prepare for the unit, Melanie designs several engaging activities for reading the graphic novel and merging content from it with textbook content. She makes liberal use of the NASA website (www.nasa.gov/audience/forstudents/5-8/index.html), with its numerous interactive options for learning and engaging content.

Melanie sets up a reading schedule of *T-Minus* that moves students through the graphic novel at a pace commensurate with the topics being covered in the textbook, other readings, and media. However, before launching into work with the book, she wisely gives her class an introduction to the graphic novel form. Without assuming that all of her students know about and have experience with this genre, she first activates her students' prior knowledge by asking them to talk about comic books they have read. Melanie writes a list of the most common ones on the whiteboard and presents students with some examples of traditional comics, such as *Superman* and *Archie*. She then explains how graphic novels are similar to these written works, as they consist of pictures and speech bubbles instead of standard paragraph-structured text. However, she emphasizes that graphic novels like *T-Minus* are normally much longer than typical comics and often deal with more complex topics and themes.

After this brief introduction, her students are issued their copies of *T-Minus*. Melanie then models techniques for reading the graphic novel. She directs the class to particular pages and reads through them with her students, showing them how to move from one text bubble to the next in the same way you would read from left to right in a standard book. She reminds her students to pause and inspect the pictures in *T-Minus* before rushing on, as much of the information present in a graphic novel is in the illustrations.

Melanie also plans experiences and assignments that will ensure that students are familiar with current lunar explorations and missions, picking up after the Apollo 11 mission, where *T-Minus* leaves off. The class textbook explains that there have been many planned, scrapped, and successful missions involving several countries, including those not traditionally associated with space exploration, such as Germany, India, and Japan. In another required reading, from *Smithsonian* magazine, Melanie's class learns that the American Lunar Reconnaissance Orbiter project is one of the most recent and important initiatives that many believe will eventually lead to establishing a human habitat on the moon's surface. To have her class inquire into this possibility, Melanie sets up an activity by first dividing students into four teams and then issuing the following premise:

> NASA's Lunar Reconnaissance Orbiter (LRO) is helping to lead us back to the moon. Already it is finding strong evidence that water exists in certain sunless areas of the moon's polar regions. Looking into the future, a number of visionary scientists have begun to draw up plans for moon-based habitats. Finding a second home in space may become increasingly urgent if our world population on Earth continues its alarming rate of growth. Based on the findings of LRO and the potential discoveries on future lunar missions, it is possible that humans could live on the moon someday. As we have learned in *T-Minus* and our other readings, since the era of intense competition between the U.S. and Soviet Union to be the first to land a man safely on the moon, space exploration has been marked by a spirit of cooperation and mutual interest. Mir and the International Space Station have opened up space science to countries from around the globe. In your teams, make plans for establishing a sustainable human habitat on the moon. Keep in mind that the people inhabiting this lunar community will bring knowledge and expertise from many different countries and cultures here on Earth.

Team One: Water and Food. A lunar colony of humans will need to be self-sustaining. It cannot rely on food and water being sent up from Earth. Research what we currently know about how these basic needs might be provided for on the moon. Explain the science involved in the technologies to produce drinkable water and edible, nutritious food. Propose your own suggestion for producing water and food on the moon and explain the science involved in this solution. What changes from those made on Earth would need to be made by colonists to ensure adequate water and food supplies?

Team Two: Dwellings and Habitat. A lunar colony of humans will need safe and adequate habitats for living. These habitats must protect humans from extreme temperatures, wind, and deadly solar radiation. They must also be comfortable and livable. Research what we currently know about how to construct moon-based dwellings for human colonization. Explain the science involved in the technologies to construct these dwellings and habitats. Propose your own suggestion for designing and building livable lunar dwellings and explain the science involved in this solution. What changes from those made on Earth would need to be made by colonists to ensure safe and comfortable living?

Team Three: Transportation. A lunar colony of humans will need durable and dependable transportation for numerous functional and scientific purposes. Research what we currently know about moon-based vehicles and what scientists envision for lunar transportation systems. Propose your own suggestion for designing and building an all-purpose lunar vehicle. What would it look like? What would it be capable of doing? What would its power source be?

Team Four: Health and Fitness. A lunar colony of humans will need to pay particular attention to issues of health and fitness on the lunar surface, where the gravitational pull is over 83% less than the earth's. Body systems can decline more rapidly and muscle loss is sped up. Research what we currently know about staying physically fit in space. Propose your own suggestion for ensuring that human colonists maintain the exercise regimen that will be necessary to stay healthy on the moon and explain the science involved in this solution.

Melanie's request that the teams render their response to the charge given them in a comic format means using an online comic generator. One option for her students is Comic Life 2 (www.plasq.com/products/comiclife2), a student-generated comic publishing program available in the school computer lab. After just a couple of tutorials and sharing a comic of her own generated with Comic Life, Melanie's students begin using it with ease. The program has been characterized as highly intuitive, requiring minimal preparation to process and produce well-polished comic creations (Pelton & Francis Pelton, 2006).

Using Comic Life 2, the four teams create a series of panels depicting the findings of their research. Some choose simple formats with explanatory narration surrounded by relevant pictures, graphics, and scenes. Other groups, mimicking the format of *T-Minus* more closely, employ the clever use of characters, dialogue and thought bubbles, and action to portray what they find. For instance, the Dwellings and Habitat team uploads photos of former president Jimmy Carter to their comic panels because of his experience and leadership in Habitat for Humanity. In this case, the team identifies him as a "lunar housing expert" who converses in dialogue bubbles with a couple of teenagers (the actual faces of two of the students on the team, with illustrated bodies using the comic generator's drawing feature). In response to questions by the teenagers, President Carter describes ideas and plans that scientists and researchers have for moon-based habitats. The teen characters then pose to Carter their own ideas about how dwellings could be built on the moon and where they might be located for maximum efficiency, such as at the lunar poles, where there is permanent sunlight.

As the student teams make reports to the class, they first describe their charge and then present their comic strips by projecting them on the whiteboard with the document camera or, if video is included, the data projector. The Transportation team devises a creative way to explain their findings. After introducing their comic, they play a short animated video of NASA's newest plan for an all-purpose solar-powered lunar vehicle, the Lunar Electric Rover, or LER. This is followed by panels created with Comic Life tools in which the LER now becomes "LERRY" and narrates how it will be a moon-dweller's "home on wheels." In appropriately illustrated moonscape scenes, LERRY describes itself as about 10 feet tall from its bed of 12 wheels to the solar reflectors on its roof. It goes on to say that the pressurized cabin features a sink, a toilet, and a collapsible exercise bike. The driver's and passenger seats are easily converted into beds, and curtains can be pulled down from the ceiling to create a separate sleeping area. LERRY excitedly describes its two hatches on the back of the cabin that allow its passengers to walk directly into dangling spacesuits, so the lunar residents can dress and exit the vehicle in a matter of minutes. Team members add to each panel brief explanations of relevant scientific principles and facts.

Melanie evaluates each team's presentation using a rubric and factors the score into the final unit grade, which also includes a couple of quizzes and a chapter test. In addition, she gathers input from the class on the graphic novel and the team activity. Her students are overwhelmingly positive about both features of this unit and urge Melanie to incorporate additional graphic novels into other science units.

Like Melanie, disciplinary teachers can support students in the creation of graphic novel panels and comics to fulfill a variety of goals, such as creating comic reinterpretations and settings for stories, poems, and plays; representing their understanding of mathematical or, in Melanie's classroom, scientific concepts; or summarizing their learning of historical events. The resulting comics can serve as one option for assessing students' knowledge of important content and ideas in the disciplines. Moreover, the best ones can be compiled into a useful and engaging resource that can be made available in paper or digital form for other students.

Introduction to Physics with Multiple Graphic Novels

As Antonio's students enter his physics class on the 1st day of school, they see written in large colorful letters on a poster above the board:

Physics is the branch of science concerned with the nature and properties of matter and energy. That includes just about everything!

This assertion is just the first of countless ways Antonio stresses to his students that concerns of physics are all around them, in the movement of the largest things we can see, planets and stars, and equally in the universe of the unseen, atoms and subatomic particles. His goal is to capture his students' imaginations about physics by demonstrating both its fascinating and mysterious as well as its practical aspects. To gain his students' attention from Day One, Antonio launches his first unit, which he calls "Stories of Physics." These are stories, he explains, because they're found in a collection of physics-related graphic novels, to which he introduces his students.

With the assistance of the school librarian, Antonio has acquired small sets of various graphic novels on topics related to physics. When using various titles within a unit, he launches the unit by introducing his students to the books through book talks (Brozo, 2010). Antonio's personal endorsement of these graphic novels by providing short, exciting glimpses with an enthusiastic delivery and expressive reading of excerpts is especially enticing to even the most reluctant reader in his class.

This year, he begins with *Feynman* (Ottaviani & Myrick, 2011). Antonio describes how the author captures the essence of the iconic Richard Feynman, a Nobel laureate in quantum physics with a quirky nature, in this vivid graphic novel. The novel not only focuses on Feynman's many scientific accomplishments, but also features his human side, the part that made him much more than an average genius. The story of his brilliance is balanced with highlights that depict him tending to his ailing wife and encouraging his younger sister to study science at a time when scientific pursuits were male-dominated fields of study.

Antonio highlights Feynman's mischievous spirit by sharing a few pages that describe how he snuck out through a hole in the fence at Los Alamos and how he astonished his colleagues with his safecracking abilities. The book takes readers through Feynman's early years when he was part of an effort to win World War II by creating the most powerful weapon in the world, the atomic bomb, to the development of his Nobel-winning theories of quantum electrodynamics to his very famous dipping of the *Challenger* O-ring material into a glass of cold water in order to demonstrate the cause of the disastrous explosion. Interjected throughout the book are vignettes that inform the reader of Feynman's sense of scientific wonder and humility and the importance that he placed on holding himself to an absolute standard of integrity.

Antonio selected this graphic novel as one of those to use in the initial unit of the school year because the storyline is very readable and the format that follows the life of this extraordinary man is very enjoyable. Antonio alerts his class to the fact that the story in the graphic novel somewhat parallels Feynman's own biography, *Surely You're Joking, Mr. Feynman* (Feynman, Leighton, Hutchings, & Hibbs, 1997). Interesting and easy to read, even the quantum theory material becomes easier to navigate with this engaging storyline. The graphic novel also employs excellent graphics, use of color, insets, and close-ups.

Antonio's introduction of *Feynman* is followed by another outstanding Ottaviani (2006) graphic novel, *Suspended in Language: Niels Bohr's Life, Discoveries, and the Century He Shaped.* This book provides a wonderful historical context and description of the life of one of quantum physics' most important scientists, Niels Bohr. Antonio demonstrates how the book offers a good balance of illustrations to keep the story interesting and the difficult subject matter digestible. He makes sure to reference the cast of scientific characters in the book, Einstein, Rutherford, Heisenberg, Pauli, and Newton, in order to help his students put the importance of Bohr's contributions into context. Antonio points out that the title of the graphic novel is significant in that it refers to how challenging it is to use language to describe the complexity of the world of subatomic particles.

The great accomplishments of Bohr's life are well covered, but Antonio hints at the descriptions of the way he was regarded by Einstein, the Nazis, and Winston Churchill, which add to the mystery of this brilliant scientist and how his scientific contributions were part of his influence on society, politics, and history. In Antonio's book talk, he makes a point of showing his students how the author, Ottaviani, while writing this interesting story of Bohr's life, does not shy away from the physics, so his students should prepare themselves to learn a quite a bit about quantum theory. Ottaviani does an excellent job of including graphics that aid the reader in understanding some of the more difficult points.

Antonio effuses over the exciting storyline, emphasizing how easy it is for the reader to be drawn into the importance of this extraordinary scientist who has had an enormous impact on modern science. Antonio displays examples of the helpful blend of graphics and text, drawing particular attention to the high-quality illustrations. The black-and-white format adds to the historical tone of the book. The index, endnotes, and references make it easy for students to navigate the novel.

Next, Antonio shares with his students *Introducing Relativity: A Graphic Guide* (Bassett & Edney, 2005). This black-and-white graphic novel begins by introducing the reader to some of the major contributors to Einstein's theory of relativity, Kant, Kepler, Newton, Maxwell, Bohr, Schrodinger, and Planck. The novel gives a very technical and detailed description of Einstein's theory of relativity, which is commonly known by his famous formula $E = mc^2$, which established the relationship between energy and mass.

Antonio draws students' attention to the novel's well-illustrated course through Einstein's thought experiments as they relate to our current understanding of modern physics, with scientists from Newton to Hawking adding their unique contributions to this story. The book traverses Einstein's views of gravity as the curvature of the space-time continuum and the relationship to the mathematics that supported his theories. Antonio points out how the author puts the importance of Einstein's discoveries into perspective by relating them to important concepts that are studied in current physics such as black holes, dark energy, and string theory.

The storyline is factual in nature and discusses complex material that is well supported by the illustrations. Even though there is a good deal of technical information in the graphic novel, the author makes it accessible to readers by providing helpful background information on important historical scientific contributions and ample black-and-white illustrations, as well as a detailed index for locating specific topics.

Antonio's next brief book talk is over *The Manga Guide to Relativity* (Yamamoto et al., 2011). Antonio knows that some of his students are already manga devotees, so he includes this classic Japanese manga-style book that effectively explains the difficult topic of relativity in an entertaining format. As with the other manga series, Antonio plays up the catchy storyline and interesting characters that will draw them into the topic. In this story, the student body president, Minagi, is challenged by the schoolmaster to study advanced physics in summer school. As boring as summer school may seem, with the help of his attractive teacher, Miss Uraga, Minagi successfully completes the course. The course that he is challenged to take tackles many difficult physics topics, including the differences between general and special relativity. Other topics that are covered include the space-time continuum, the effects on a body when approaching the speed of light, the derivation of Einstein's famed $E = mc^2$ equation, the relationship between energy and mass and gravity and acceleration, and black holes. Antonio demonstrates how the informative illustrations help fill in for difficult concepts. Another helpful feature is that each chapter contains a detailed technical section filled with deeper explorations of the chapter's subject.

Characters in *The Manga Guide to Relativity* make for a very engaging story-line that Antonio knows will keep his students reading through difficult scientific content. Strength of storyline gives purpose and motivation to learning content material. He also selected this manga graphic novel because the technical information is very well presented through both text and illustrations, making the content easier to understand. The book is in the classic black-and-white Japanese manga style that includes helpful chapter summaries to provide background information and reinforce the most important concepts.

The final graphic novel in the group is Nitta and Takastu's (2010) *The Manga Guide to Physics.* In this book talk, Antonio plays up the plot in this classic manga graphic novel, which revolves around a high school tennis star, Megumi, who is frustrated by both her game and her physics class. She befriends a classmate, Ryota, who is anxious to help her with physics, and she soon learns that the principles of Newton's laws of motion also apply to her tennis game. Antonio makes certain that his students appreciate that the female character's savvy tutor uses real-life examples of tennis, rollerblading, cars, and slingshots to help her understand the basic principles of physics and apply the principles to improve her tennis game. Antonio includes this manga-style graphic novel not only for the entertaining plot but also for how well it's organized. Each of the four chapters ("Law of Action and Reaction," "Force and Motion," "Momentum," and "Energy") is divided into two sections. The first part is the story of the tennis player, and the second part is referred to as "The Laboratory," which focuses on reviewing the lessons learned in the story with added detail. *The Laboratory* adds some background mathematical information (trigonometry, calculus, vectors) as well as relevant equations, graphs, and practice problems. The extended explanations, examples, and supportive graphics are helpful to the reader.

Antonio describes the book to his students as a charming story of two students on a quest to learn physics. He knows that the author's clever interactions between the main characters will hold his students' interest throughout the technical content. In addition, Antonio likes the ample examples and supportive graphics that will help his students understand the more difficult topics. The book also contains a detailed table of contents, support information on understanding the International System of Units, and an extensive index, which make this a useful reference.

When finished with giving his students personal introductions to each graphic novel, Antonio spreads the books on a table in the back of the room and invites students to browse them so they can decide which book they would like to read. He joins the class as they peruse the books, answering questions and helping to guide students who are undecided. Afterward, he identifies individual students and their book choices, thereby allowing groups to form based on student preference. As needed, he intervenes to move students into other groups to achieve the maximum of five in each.

The next important step is explaining the roles each group member will play. He begins by describing the value of cooperative learning, stressing that most real-world business, research and development, and professional environments are structured around teamwork; this is especially the case in STEM-related fields (Ho & Boo, 2007). Antonio knows that for cooperative groups to function effectively, it is very important to assign roles to students that are unambiguous and contribute positively to the whole group (Peterson & Miller, 2004). He creates roles for his students that past experience has told him would achieve these goals; however, he realizes that equally effective groups might be formed with alternative roles and assignments. The key is that each individual member makes a contribution that relates to the purpose of the group work and improves the performance of the group overall (Hancock, 2004; Reveles, Cordova, & Kelly, 2004).

The roles Antonio describes and demonstrates are designed to maximize how and what his students have processed from each of their graphic novels. Thus, the "text evidencer" is responsible for generating important ideas that could be linked directly to what the author and illustrator presented. The "science linguist" gathers science-related terminology from the book and provides understandable definitions for the group. The "discussion director" presents issues to the group derived from what they were reading in the graphic novel and prompts conversation around these issues. The "skeptic" has to find corroborative evidence for controversial or challenging facts and assertions. The "presenter" is responsible for sharing with the whole class the big ideas and other relevant information from the group that they have derived from reading and studying their graphic novel.

Antonio also explains that students will become familiar with every role, as these will rotate each class session during this opening unit on physics. Each cooperative learning role is accompanied by a form to be filled out by the student assuming that role on a given day. In this way, Antonio holds students accountable for their level of engagement, learning, and cooperation.

To manage classroom activities and pacing of content with five different graphic novels and cooperative groups, Antonio employs a creative system developed over several years of similar teaching methods. Each group is given a reading schedule that includes the page numbers to be completed for each class session of the unit. To keep each group progressing at a similar pace, the number of pages required varies based on the length and density of the book. Also, overarching questions and discussion prompts are presented to all the groups. These serve to tie together information and ideas from each book and connect the content to the unit's purpose—to initiate students into the discipline of physics through stories.

To illustrate how Antonio manages the physics classroom with multiple graphic novels, let's look at the activities he and his students in their cooperative groups engage in for 1 day. In this 90-minute block, students enter the classroom, find their graphic novels stacked on the table in the back of the room, and look over the printed reading schedule on the wall next to the table and the cooperative learning role rotation for that day. Tory finds her graphic novel, *The Manga Guide to Physics*, sees that she is assigned the role of "science linguist," takes that form from the pile of handouts, and returns to her seat to begin reading. Tory has selected this book because she already enjoys reading manga-style graphic novels and the main character is a teenage girl who is an athlete struggling with physics. Tory is on the high school soccer team and worries that physics will be too difficult for her, even though she was advised into the class to better prepare for college.

As Tory reads and studies the manga-style illustrations, she pays particular attention to physics-related terminology she thinks she and her group members need to know. She encounters the term "aerodynamic drag" in reference to the physics concepts Megumi's tutor, Ryota, is trying to teach her and the kinds of tennis shots she is trying to learn. Tory writes this term on her sheet and consults the physics textbook's glossary for a definition, which offers that it's when the force of air on an object resists the object's motion. Tory also provides an example of the term, in this case, how far a goalie can kick a soccer ball down the field when the air is thick and muggy versus when the air is thin on a bright crisp day. As she reads on, she adds other vocabulary words like "momentum" and "parabolic motion" to her sheet, along with definitions and examples.

During the same time Tory is reading and working, her group's other members are similarly engaged with the same set of required pages and filling out a sheet for their cooperative learning roles. After 15 minutes or so, Antonio asks students to finish reading and gather in their groups. Tables spread throughout the room make it convenient for the five cooperative learning groups to cluster separately and comfortably. Antonio urges group members to organize themselves so they can participate in normal face-to-face conversation. As his class gets settled, he moves from group to group to check in, stimulate dialogue, offer clarifications to roles and book content, and answer any questions.

Once Tory's group gathers at its table, the members decide to begin with a consideration of new vocabulary. Tory shares the terms recorded on the science linguist sheet (see Figure 5.1), physics-related terms extracted from the section of required reading in *The Manga Guide to Physics*. Based on Antonio's modeling, Tory knows she is not supposed to "give away" the definitions and examples of the words outright, but encourage the group to use strategies and processes for determining their meanings.

Beginning with "aerodynamic drag," Tory directs her group partners to the page, paragraph, and sentence in which the term first appears. She reads aloud, then asks the others to consider how the remaining context and

Figure 5.1. Science Linguist Recording Sheet

SCIENCE LINGUIST

Name: Tory

Reading Assignment: pp. 7–16 of *The Manga Guide to Physics*

Date: 2/16/13

Word	Page	Definition	Example
aerodynamic drag	8	when the force of air on an object resists the object's motion	Soccer goalie can't kick the ball as far in humid weather versus dry weather.
momentum	9	the ability of an object to keep its state of motion	The mass and velocity of a soccer ball kicked toward the goal is its momentum.
parabolic motion	12	the path of any object that is launched	A kicked soccer ball moves up in the air against gravity then falls in a loop to the ground because of gravity.
Newtonian mechanics	14	the relationship between force, mass, and motion	A soccer ball remains still until kicked; force of a soccer ball on a players head is equal on both the ball and the head

illustrations help give clues to the meaning. Next, she invites suggestions for gaining certainty about and further refining the definition. Members suggest reading other related pages in the graphic novel, consulting the glossary in their physics textbook, and looking it up on the Internet. Tory then reads the meaning of "aerodynamic drag" she has written on her sheet and the others further refine the definition using the textbook and the Internet. Once the group agrees on the final definition, Tory asks for applications of the term, sharing hers as an example. Other group members suggest that aerodynamic drag is at play when one tries to fly a kite on a calm day or throw a football against a strong wind.

Tory's group repeats this process with the other physics-related words she identified from the graphic novel. Once the science linguist's work is concluded, the others take the lead, helping to focus on the ideas and supporting information in the required section of text, challenging the team with questions about physics' assumptions and laws, and prompting discussion over various issues that emerged from the graphic novel. All the while, the student in the group who is the presenter for that day takes notes on the group's deliberations and prepares them for sharing with the whole class.

After a total of about 15 minutes of cooperative group work, Antonio begins calling on the presenters to report to the class. Today, as with previous sessions in this first unit of the new school year, Antonio requests that presenters focus their brief reports on what they learned about physics from their graphic novels. As students present, Antonio writes the prominent facts and ideas about physics on the board.

The *Feynman* group presenter recounts Feynman's contribution to the building of the first atomic bomb and his theory of quantum electrodynamics, which describes how light and matter interact and brings together theories of quantum mechanics and special relativity. Reporting on its graphic novel about Niels Bohr, the group's presenter says that their reading for the day also had information about Bohr's contribution to the atomic bomb, bringing in his knowledge about quantum mechanics and the understanding of the special behavior of subatomic matter. The next group's presenter shares what was learned in their day's reading of *Introducing Relativity: A Graphic Guide*. Because Antonio scheduled group readings in such a way as to ensure that as many common topics were being encountered across the books as possible, the physics-related content highlighted is Einstein's famous equation $E = mc^2$, which posits that energy equals matter times the speed of light squared. Also cited is string theory, an outgrowth of Einstein's theory of relativity that attempts to explain all particles and fundamental forces of nature in one unified theory. *The Manga Guide to Relativity* group's presenter immediately follows and talks about how the members learned about Einstein's special theory of relativity, which explains the relative motion of two objects moving at the same constant speed. The final group to present is Tory's, using *The Manga Guide to Physics*, and the relationship between mass and force is briefly described.

At the conclusion of the group presenters' reports, Antonio draws the students' attention to the board, where he has written the key terms and essential ideas from each graphic novel that day. He tells students they will be exploring in greater detail in his class over the course of the year theories and applications of mass, force, and energy; the behavior of subatomic particles; and relativity.

As a closure activity, Antonio asks students to turn toward their cooperative group members and reflect on the level and quality of participation by each of them. Antonio reminds the class to base their reflections on the key features of effective cooperative learning he has gone over with them throughout the unit: (1) individual accountability, (2) appropriate use of collaborative skills, and (3) constructive face-to-face interaction. Students comment on the effectiveness of their group process and how much they enjoy reading the physics-related graphic novels and how much they are learning from these books.

LOOKING BACK AND MOVING FORWARD

In this chapter, we discovered the value of integrating graphic novels into the science curriculum. We began with a research rationale for using graphic novels and comics to teach science. This was followed by a description of instructional practices and strategies for increasing students' motivation for and learning of disciplinary content in the sciences. Three approaches used by science teachers in secondary schools were described and exemplified, including reading aloud from a single graphic novel, employing instructional practices with one graphic novel for each student, and managing multiple graphic novels within a cooperative learning format. In each case, the teachers took full advantage of the graphic novels to gain and sustain students' attention, build knowledge, and support disciplinary literacy.

In the next chapter, you will encounter math teachers, who, like the science teachers in this chapter, exploit the motivational, literacy learning, and knowledge-building potential of thematically and topically related graphic novels.

Study Group Questions for Chapter 5

- In your role as a teacher or teacher leader, what are some specific steps you can take to enrich the professional resources for science teachers in your school with graphic novels?
- What are the pros and cons of using graphic novels in your school's science curriculum? What can be done to convince your science colleagues of the benefits of using graphic novels in their instruction?
- In your role as a teacher or teacher leader, how can you ensure that science teachers receive supportive professional development in instructional practices with graphic novels?

CHAPTER SIX

Using Graphic Novels to Teach Math

ANTICIPATION GUIDE

Directions: Read each statement carefully and decide whether you agree or disagree with it, placing a check mark in the appropriate Before Reading column. When you have finished reading and studying Chapter 6, return to the guide and decide whether your anticipations need to be changed by placing a check mark in the appropriate After Reading column.

	BEFORE READING		AFTER READING	
	Agree	*Disagree*	*Agree*	*Disagree*
1. Math teachers may struggle with the idea of teaching with graphic novels.				
2. Graphic novels can help move math instruction from memorization to inquiry and applied problem-solving.				
3. Math graphic novels are helpful learning aids because they repeat what is in the textbook.				
4. Some topics like calculus are not covered by graphic novels.				
5. Because youth find math-related graphic novels interesting and fun to read, they are more likely to learn from them.				

The Texture of Reality

Nature deals in non-uniform shapes and rough edges. Take the human form. There is a certain symmetry about it, but it is, and has always been, indescribable in terms of Euclidean geometry. It is not a uniform shape. This is the issue. What has been missing from the scientific repertoire until very recently has been a way of describing the shapes and objects of the real world.

This panel from the first few pages of *Introducing Fractals: A Graphic Guide* (Lesmoir-Gordon, Rood, & Edney, 2009), with its clever illustrations and informative text, demonstrates the value of graphic novels, for helping to make complex concepts, such as fractals, accessible to students in math.

> Connecting literature in the form of pictures with math is not only beneficial to students' math learning, but it can serve as a form of motivation, as well.
>
> —Cara M. Halpern and Pamela A. Halpern,
> "Using Creative Writing and Literature in Mathematics Class"

IN A RECENT VISIT TO A high school mathematics class, we witnessed a routine that was reminiscent of our own high school math classes many years before. Students came in, found their seats, and put their homework on their desks. The teacher walked up and down the rows with his grade book, looking at student work and recording marks. Afterward, he went to the board and explained the correct way to solve a couple of problems that several students had gotten incorrect.

The teacher asked if there was still any confusion, and no one responded. It was as if there were an understanding among class members that to ask questions meant more time for teacher explanation and less time to work in class on their homework, which would be given before long. The teacher next handed out a worksheet with several problems that students were to solve on their own. After about 10 minutes, the teacher worked out answers on the board or called a couple of students up to work them out. Inevitably, these were the most capable ones, who seemed to have the process and answers correct. The others in the class were expected to check their own answers, though it appeared that many simply copied the solutions from the board. About 10 minutes before the end of the period, homework was assigned—solve all the even-numbered problems at the end of the chapter. Some began work right away, while others visited quietly with a friend. The teacher stayed at his desk to help individual students who came to him for assistance until the bell rang and the class hastily filed out.

We thanked the teacher for inviting us in and said our good-byes. In a debriefing session afterward, we focused on the support we might provide this teacher and others like him who have fallen into what has become a common pattern in this era of high-stakes testing and teacher accountability—covering content but not teaching students.

Whether this all-too-typical kind of math instruction is having an adverse effect on student performance is debatable. One might find that the situation is not that serious, given the results of the most recent Trends in International Math and Science Study (TIMSS) (Mullis, Martin, Foy, & Arora, 2011), which positions U.S. 8th-graders overall slightly above the average internationally. However, this level of achievement is far below that of the real winners, such as Singapore, Japan, and Korea. And on the National Assessment of Educational Progress (NAEP) in math, while long-term gains have been made, too many of our 8th-grade students, especially low-income and minority students, continue to perform at very basic levels (NCES, 2011).

Perhaps the more significant question is whether the ways in which many students in the United States learn math adequately prepare them for the demands of life, work, and society in the 21st century. "Routine expertise" (Bill & Jamar, 2010, p. 64), of the kind being inculcated by the math teacher we observed, may be insufficient for today's youth. To be prepared for tomorrow's workplace, Pellegrino (2006) asserts, students need "adaptive expertise," or levels of knowledge and understanding that can support transfer to new problems, creativity and "innovation" (pp. 1–2). Thus, in addition to learning facts, concepts, skills, procedures, and notations, students of mathematics should also develop the capacity for generative ways of thinking that lead to expanded understandings and solutions to new problems (Bill & Jamar, 2010).

We would like to propose a vision for mathematical teaching and learning that moves beyond routine knowledge to something closer to socially constructed mathematical inquiry. This kind of learning is possible, according to Goos (2004), in classroom communities where discussion and collaboration are supported, where students freely propose and defend mathematical conjectures and are encouraged to respond critically to mathematical assertions of their classmates, and where finding and correcting errors in their own and others' thinking is valued. Furthermore, we propose a community of inquiry wherein mathematical literacy and language are braided together into a tightly woven instructional strand in order to make the content and process of math accessible and engaging to all students (Brozo & Simpson, 2007).

Over a decade ago, the National Council of Teachers of Mathematics (2000) had this to say about the important connections between math and literacy: "Students who have opportunities, encouragement, and support for writing, reading, and listening in mathematics classes reap dual benefits: they communicate to learn mathematics, and they learn to communicate mathematically" (p. 60). The Common Core has created a new urgency to find ways of developing disciplinary literacy for youth in all the subject areas, including math. Meanwhile, others have been exploring the benefits of graphic novels and comics in math (Pelton & Pelton, 2009; Toh, 2009). These resources can help fulfill the dual function the NCTM recognized in that they create opportunities for students to read about math in an interesting and engaging medium while learning math concepts, processes, and facts (Halimun, 2011; Kessler, 2009; Sengul, 2011).

Although the nexus of mathematics and literacy is where graphic novels should be found, we have known some math teachers who characterized themselves as purists who would probably find the idea of using graphic novels and comics to teach their subject matter far-fetched or even a waste of time. After all, time is a precious commodity in math class, especially given how much content must be covered in a typical math curriculum. And yet we also know many other math teachers who successfully weave reading and writing processes into their math curriculum without sacrificing content. The admonishments and instructional suggestions in this chapter are for both types of teachers, because we believe both types will reap the benefits of heightened student engagement in math learning, increased student participation in math activities, and greater student enjoyment of learning math when graphic novels and comics are woven into the curriculum.

INSTRUCTIONAL PRACTICES
WITH GRAPHIC NOVELS IN MATH

Exploring the Strange World
of Fractals in High School Geometry

In Latiffe's inquiry-oriented geometry class, students use reading for a variety of purposes similar to those identified by Siegel and Fonzi (1995): reading to comprehend, to remember, to get an example, to generate something new, and to make public. Thus, her students always learn postulates, theorems, and formulas through reading, writing, and real-life parallels.

Latiffe has acquired several fiction and nonfiction books over the past few years that allow her students to make connections to the content. For example, when teaching ways of measuring three-dimensional objects, Latiffe introduces her class to the study of geometry by reading aloud from *The Planiverse* (Dewdney, 1984). This peculiar novel describes how the author, A. K. Dewdney, and his computer science students, as they are working on the design of a vertical two-dimensional world, find that their artificial 2-D universe has somehow accidentally become a means of communication with an actual 2-D world called Arde. The students make telepathic contact with Yendred, a resident of Arde. As Yendred journeys across a continent of his world, he reveals to the students, through thoughts that show up as words on a computer printout, the politics, geography, and even building construction of Arde. Latiffe also makes copies of a follow-up article by Dewdney (2000) titled "The Planiverse Project: Then and Now," which adds graphic details about the Arde, including how the laws of gravity behave in a 2-D environment and what fish and vehicles look like on a planiverse, as well as how to navigate waters and produce a steam engine.

Latiffe has found that stories, articles, and books can be incorporated into her geometry course without sacrificing any essential content, while at the same time raising the interest level and attention of her students. More recently, she has acquired graphic novels that fit into the curriculum. One such novel she uses in conjunction with a unit on how to measure naturally occurring shapes is *Introducing Fractals: A Graphic Guide* (Lesmoir-Gordon et al., 2009).

Latiffe likes this graphic novel because it opens with a history of the development of fractal theory. The authors introduce the many contributors to the field of fractals, including scientists such as Kepler, Newton, Heisenberg, and Mandelbrot. The origins of fractal geometry are well explained in the novel, beginning with Euclidian geometry, calculus, and the paradox of infinitesimals, then continuing on to the discovery of the first mathematical fractal, discovered in 1871 by Karl Weierstrass, through the important works of Mandelbrot.

As the authors of the graphic novel explain, the origin of the word *fractal* is attributed to Benoit Mandelbrot, a Polish French American mathematician who coined the phrase from the Latin word *fractus,* meaning broken and discontinuous. The authors go on to define fractal geometry as an extension of classical geometry, but much more powerful because it allows scientists and mathematicians to describe irregular objects with geometric precision. Latiffe has noticed that the complex subject matter, given such a meaningful and thought-provoking treatment by the authors and illustrator, can instill a sense of wonder in the way her students begin to view the natural world.

The word *fractal* was coined in order to describe shapes of all scales. Like Latiffe's approach to the subject, the novel contrasts the shapes of the natural world and its chaotic nature with the ideal forms of Euclidian geometry, which her students have already studied at the point she introduces this book.

The story line is factual in nature, with some humor interjected throughout the novel. The book closes with the implications and applications of fractal geometry with a helpful list of suggested readings to explore.

Although the technical information on fractals is dense, the authors provide needed background information on important historical scientific contributors, with in-depth discussion and explicit description of the concepts. There are ample black-and-white illustrations that make the technical information and concepts accessible. The book also includes a detailed index that is helpful in locating specific topics.

Latiffe begins the first lesson of the unit on fractals by reading statements from the speech balloons of two of the current leading thinkers on fractals, John Archibald Wheeler and Ian Stewart, both illustrated in the graphic novel, as she projects the page on the whiteboard with the document camera.

> *Wheeler*: No one will be considered scientifically literate tomorrow who is
>   not familiar with fractals. (p. 3)
> *Stewart*: Fractals are important because they reveal a new area of
>   mathematics directly relevant to the study of nature. (p. 3)

Students are then instructed to open their geometry texts to the chapter on fractals, where they read together that fractal geometry is not just the study of complex shapes and interesting computer-generated pictures. They learn that fractals can be any shape that is random and irregular and, thus, are everywhere in our lives, showing up in places as small as a cell's membrane and as large as the vastness of the solar system. They learn further that fractals are the unique, irregular patterns that result from unpredictable movements in the natural world. Latiffe then directs the class's attention to the graphic novel again and reads a speech bubble for the illustrated Benoit Mandelbrot, considered the father of modern fractal theory, who says in the book: "Uniform rectangular objects like boxes and buildings do not appear in nature" (p. 5).

She goes on to read from the graphic novel:

> The world that we live in is not naturally smooth-edged. The real world has been fashioned with rough edges. Smooth surfaces are the exception in nature. And yet, we have accepted a geometry that only describes shapes rarely—if ever—found in the real world. The geometry of Euclid describes ideal shapes—the sphere, the circle, the cube, the square. Now these shapes do occur in our lives, but they are mostly man-made and not nature-made. (p. 5)

Latiffe asks students to turn to a neighbor and think of things in their everyday life that might constitute a fractal. As students discuss and brainstorm ideas, Latiffe moves through the room to monitor, clarify, and provide feedback. Afterward, she invites student suggestions and, as they're received, writes them on the board. The list of examples includes

- the branching of tracheal tubes
- leaves in trees
- veins in a hand
- water swirling and twisting out of a tap
- a puffy cumulus cloud
- the DNA molecule
- a meteor
- a lightning bolt
- the stock market
- mold growing in the showers of the boys' locker room
- wrinkles on an unpressed school uniform shirt
- us, humans

In theory, then, Latiffe tells the class, turning to the graphic novel again, virtually everything in the world is a fractal, as she reads: "Fractal geometry is a new language. Once you speak it, you can describe the shape of a cloud as precisely as an architect a house!" (p. 8). So, she says, let's see if we can learn to speak the language of fractal geometry.

Switching back to the textbook, the class discovers that the study of fractals is more than just a new field in science that unifies mathematics, theoretical physics, art, and computer science. It is the discovery of a new geometry, one that describes the boundless universe we live in, one that is in constant motion, not as static images in books. Today, many scientists are trying to find applications for fractal geometry, from predicting stock market prices to making new discoveries in theoretical physics.

As the unit progresses and Latiffe continues to read from *Introducing Fractals* in and around reading assignments she gives her class from the geometry textbook, she prepares students for a culminating activity involving research into real-world applications of fractal geometry. Students learn from the graphic novel about the ever-increasing applications of fractals in science and medicine. This growing use is attributed to fractals' ability to describe the real world better than do traditional mathematics and physics.

Latiffe requires her students to select one of the areas where fractal geometry is being applied, according to the graphic novel, and research specific ways it is and will be used in that field and the current and future job opportunities that result. Students work with a partner on this project, and after one week of planning give a PowerPoint presentation of their findings to the class.

Astronomy. Isaac and Rickey report that fractals have the potential to revolutionize the way that the universe is studied. They state that astronomers used to assume that matter is equally distributed across space. Recent observations with new space telescopes show that this is not true. Many astronomers, they say, still think that the universe is smooth at very large scales. However, another group of scientists claims that the structure of the universe is fractal at all scales, small and large. If this new theory is proved to be correct, the presenters go on to report, even the Big Bang models about the origin of the universe may need to be adapted.

Isaac and Rickey report on additional interesting facts about the relationship between fractals and astronomy. The most significant finding they share is that galaxy structures are highly irregular and self-similar (i.e., the whole has the same shape as one or more of the parts). This means, they discovered, that the usual statistical methods for measuring on an astronomical scale, which have been based on the assumption of homogeneity of matter across the universe, are therefore inconsistent. A new breed of astrophysicists and astronomers say there is a need for a more general, conceptual framework to identify the real physical properties of these galactic structures. But at present, Isaac and Rickey conclude, cosmologists need more data about how matter is distributed throughout space to prove that we are living in a fractal universe.

Based on their research, Rickey and Isaac say that there are jobs with NASA requiring understanding of fractal geometry to help explain anomalous redshift data (i.e., a method for determining distances of objects in space) from space telescopes.

Nature. Linda and Maria take up the topic of fractals in nature as identified in *Introducing Fractals*. They introduce the topic by showing a short video clip from the episode of the PBS program *Nova* titled "Hunting the Hidden Dimension" (aired October 18, 2008; Davis, Hobson, Jersey, & Schwartz, 2008). The program opens with pictures of bizarre colorful patterns while the narrator intones:

> Mysteriously beautiful fractals are shaking up the world of mathematics and deepening our understanding of nature. You can find it in the rainforest, on the frontiers of medical research, in the movies, and it's all over the world of wireless communications. One of nature's biggest design secrets has finally been revealed. It's an odd-looking shape you may never have heard of, but it's everywhere around you: the jagged repeating form called a fractal. For centuries, fractal-like irregular shapes were considered beyond the boundaries of mathematical understanding. Now, mathematicians have finally begun mapping this uncharted territory.

The two girls then pick up from there and invite their classmates to consider a tree as an example. Using PowerPoint slides of a tree and then a branch from the tree, they ask everyone to study them closely. Then they show a bundle of leaves from the branch for the class to observe. All of these objects, they say—the tree, the branch, and the leaves—are the same, according to fractal geometricians. Do you agree, they ask their classmates? Some say they see the pattern; others do not.

Linda and Maria point out that finding these elusive and intricate patterns in nature is a big part of what is involved in fractal geometry. One purpose of studying patterns that appear irregular and dynamic through fractals is to predict patterns in a system that seems unpredictable. A system in nature, they go on to say, is a set of things, such as how clouds form, how weather changes, how water currents move, or the way animals migrate. The girls focus on weather as an ideal example of predicting patterns in a dynamic system. With colorful photos of rainstorms and tornadoes on their slides, they state that weather forecasters can never be completely accurate; and the longer the range of the forecast, the greater the error. This is because, they point out, small changes in factors such as wind direction and solar heating will change weather outcomes over time so that they will be far different than what was predicted.

With fractal geometry, the girls report, we can visually model much of what we witness in nature, including the weather, but also structures like coastlines and mountains. They add other examples of how fractals are used, such as predicting soil erosion and analyzing seismic patterns. They conclude by stating that everything about Mother Nature is fractal.

Regarding career opportunities in fractal geometry related to their topic, they refer back to the PBS program and describe the work of mathematicians who are using fractals to better understand the rainforests and predict their evolution given use and conservation patterns.

Other pairs of students in Latiffe's geometry class present on fractal applications in computer science, for processes such as image compression that is much more refined than JPEG or GIF file formats; fluid mechanics, for the study of complex and chaotic turbulent flows of air, fire, and fluids such as oil and oil by-products used in petroleum science; telecommunications, with new reduced-size fractal-shaped antennae; medicine, where fractals are being used to study biosensors as in blood glucose sensors; and even the fashion design and textile industries, where fractal geometry is inspiring creative new patterns for clothes and textiles based on computer-generated fractal algorithms, citing a leading fashion designer, Jhane Barnes, whose patterns are appearing on menswear, footwear, and carpets.

Once the unit on fractals is complete and Latiffe has finished reading aloud *Introducing Fractals: A Graphic Guide*, she makes the graphic novel available to any of her geometry students to read individually. She has observed that the books she reads to the class are eagerly sought after by many students so they can enjoy them again on their own and absorb the content at their own pace.

An Introduction to Calculus with Manga

Darnell emphasizes to his middle school students in his mathematics classes that he wants them to develop habits of thinking like mathematicians. Above the board at the front of the room is a poster with a quote from a favorite professional book: "A 'Habit of Mind' means having a disposition toward behaving intelligently when confronted with problems, the answers to which are not immediately known" (Costa & Kallick, 2000, p. 15). This is followed by his list of the most highly valued habits of mind, including Persisting, Thinking Flexibly, Striving for Accuracy and Precision, Questioning and Posing Problems, Communicating with Clarity, Gathering Data Through All Senses, Thinking Interdependently, and Learning Continuously. Virtually every day, Darnell reminds his students of the importance of these characteristics and points out when they are being enacted by someone during math lessons.

Darnell also tells his students, many of whom in this urban multicultural school have to work constantly to overcome low academic self-esteem, that his is a "zero failure" classroom, meaning that he expects everyone to achieve at a high level and is always there to support student achievement. A supportive classroom context is especially critical when studying challenging mathematical content, such as calculus, which Darnell introduces to his 8th-graders with the expectation that they will develop competency, applying it to academic and real-world problems. However, Darnell also knows from experience with and sensitivity to the needs of students in his school that along with holding high expectations, teachers should scaffold youth to meet these expectations with engaging instructional practices and texts.

An engaging text Darnell has been using to help teach calculus, which is the mathematical study of change, is *The Manga Guide to Calculus* (Kojima & Togami, 2010). Darnell has found that this book, illustrated in classic black-and-white Japanese manga style, serves as an excellent accompanying text and introduction to calculus for his middle-graders. One of the many strengths of this book is the manner in which it sets a context for using calculus, which Darnell knows his students desperately need in order to find a connection to the content. The authors do this by establishing a story line about a young, ambitious newspaper reporter who is assigned to an area where she is not likely to find many high-profile news opportunities. The focus of the story turns when she learns that her bureau chief is a calculus enthusiast. Much to her surprise, she discovers that she can use calculus to help her explore trends in data that provide her with stories of interest that may have otherwise been overlooked without its aid.

Having a context in which to conceptualize the difficult mathematical concepts introduced in calculus is a welcome format for Darnell's students. Instead of introducing his students to the concept of calculus via the mechanics of performing mathematical calculations, Darnell ensures that they also understand the usefulness of calculus in solving problems and answering important questions. The story line of the graphic novel does what Darnell's own class textbook cannot do: It provides motivation to learn more about the subject.

Although a large number of concepts are covered in the graphic novel, the fairly shallow depth of coverage makes the content accessible to even Darnell's struggling students. In addition to the large number of topics covered, practice exercises are provided in each section, with solutions at the back of the book. The practice exercises serve as a good way for Darnell's students to check their understanding of calculus topics presented in the graphic novel.

The characters in this manga-style graphic novel make for a very engaging story line, and the technical information, which is well presented and integrated, keeps Darnell's students interested while presenting difficult mathematical content. The strength of the story line gives purpose to and motivates learning about calculus from the book. Darnell is especially impressed with the illustrations used to explain calculus concepts and processes. The table of contents and index increase the reader-friendly nature of the graphic novel.

Darnell obtained a class set of *The Manga Guide to Calculus* with funds he received for a small grant from his district's teacher foundation. To ensure that students are experiencing the graphic novel on a regular basis, Darnell builds in

10–15 minutes of sustained silent reading (SSR) time into each math lesson. SSR has been found to be a critical facet in a comprehensive literacy program (Garan & DeVoogd, 2008; Gardiner, 2005; Yoon, 2002) and may be particularly helpful to youth in urban school settings (Fisher & Frey, 2008; Francois, 2013).

Darnell learned about SSR as a result of participating the previous year in a teacher study group at his school sponsored by the principal and reading specialist. The school's focus was on improving students' reading and writing achievement, so all teachers were enlisted in the effort. He and several colleagues from a range of subject areas read and discussed *The SSR Handbook: How to Organize and Manage a Sustained Silent Reading Program* (Pilgreen, 2000). He learned about Pilgreen's factors that contribute to successful SSR programs (see Figure 6.1) and explored ways with his colleagues how he could make room in his math class for some form of SSR based on the guidelines.

In connection to his unit on calculus, Darnell creates *access* by making an *appealing* and informative graphic novel available to each student. To create a more genial atmosphere in his classroom, he reorganized the desks and tables to make the *environment* more comfortable for students to read independently or, for some who need more interaction during SSR time, to talk with a partner about the book. Darnell always *encourages* his students to adopt the habits of mind he supports generally for the books and texts they read during SSR. He does this by modeling ways of reading and thinking about the graphic novel and fostering questioning, discussion, and application of new understandings after each SSR session. Although Darnell neither requires formal book reports nor gives tests about the graphic novel's content, he takes advantage of a variety of other informal ways his students are *held accountable* for what they read and learn from the book. He ensures students have *follow-up experiences* based on the graphic novel that will sustain their interest in the topic and in reading about it. Finally, by creating 10–15 minutes of SSR time in each class, Darnell is ensuring that his

Figure 6.1. Pilgreen's Factors That Contribute to Successful SSR Programs

- Access
- Appeal
- Environment
- Encouragement
- Nonaccountability
- Follow-Up Activities
- Distributed Time to Read

students have the needed *print experience over time* to positively affect their reading attitudes and skills and increase their knowledge of math through reading.

To better appreciate Darnell's mathematics classroom at work, we'll take a closer look. It begins this morning period with his 24 students passing through the open door, where he waits to greet them as they enter. He receives fist bumps and other acknowledgments, joining some in a bit of small talk about the school's sports teams and other school and personal news. Students grab a copy of the graphic novel and find a comfortable chair or sprawl on the floor. Once everyone is in and Darnell closes the door, he draws their attention to the page numbers written on the board, and then asks them to begin reading for the next 15 minutes. Darnell has set an achievable page-limit goal for most of his students. Some can read ahead, while others, specifically the more challenged readers and English language learners, move more slowly through the graphic novel or can read with a partner. Darnell also reads from *The Manga Guide to Calculus* during this SSR time, though he keeps his eyes open for any flagrant off-task behavior or requests for assistance.

When SSR time is up, Darnell asks students to form groups of four, which creates six groups in this class. As he demonstrates, Darnell tells each group to fold a sheet of paper into four quadrants (Fisher, Zike, & Frey, 2007; see Figure 6.2). He then points to the interactive whiteboard, where he has written a calculus problem for each group related to the pages the class has just read in the graphic novel. The problems today have to do with functions, or how changes in one variable affect another. Darnell has found that students are motivated to learn how to graph functions, figure out why they look the way they do, and learn the math and algebra skills necessary to manipulate the formulas if they are applied to solving real-world problems. Motivation to learn topics such as

Figure 6.2. Discussion Sheet Quadrants

Visualize It	Proposed Solution
Check It	Explain It

calculus is also heightened when one of the critical text sources is a book like *The Manga Guide to Calculus*, with its fun story line that is embedded with calculus problems.

Darnell's problems for the groups to solve include having a playlist of songs and choosing some to fill an 80-minute blank CD-R as full as they can; having $100 and a couple of coupons totaling $14, then figuring out how to buy the most stuff at a store; throwing a party and taking a brownie recipe described in fractions and making enough batches for a large number of guests; finding the cost of trash removal in the year 2020 for a town growing in population according to an exponential function of time; determining the average price of houses in the student's community over the next 5 years based on changing population patterns; and predicting the price of a company's stock in July based on a yearly graph of prices.

Because Darnell has difficulty finding problems like this in the math textbook, he spends a considerable amount of time generating them himself. The effort is well worth it, as he observes his students going beyond conversations about correct answers to questions about why certain decisions were made in the process of solving problems.

As the groups work to solve their own calculus problems, each student in the group assumes responsibility for a specific role:

- Drawing a visual representation of the problem and solution.
- Proposing a way of solving the problem and defending it.
- Proposing a method of checking the proposed solution.
- Explaining the process and proposed solution to the class.

Individual members of the group take the lead on their assigned role, engaging the others in conversation and brainstorming. After the groups allow time for each member to provide input in a roundtable discussion format (Fisher, Brozo, Frey, & Ivey, in press), members fill out their assigned quadrant on the discussion sheet. Darnell invites the spokesperson from each group to write his or her proposed solution on the interactive whiteboard and explain the group's reasoning. The rest of the class is encouraged to ask questions and critique their peers' process of solving the problem. In this way, the students learn to defend their reasoning and learn from suggestions on alternative paths to getting the solution.

To ensure that his students fully understand the critical content in *The Manga Guide to Calculus* and to reinforce appropriate habits of mind, Darnell interacts with students to model and elicit close reading practices. Close reading is an instructional approach that focuses readers' attention on what an author is saying as the basis for more meaningful and expansive interpretations or applications. This kind of detailed, repeated reading is warranted for more complex and foundational content (Fisher, Frey, & Lapp, 2012; Newkirk, 2010) and is a linchpin of the new Common Core English/language arts standards (Boyles, 2012/2013).

Darnell directs his students' attention to pages 9 and 10 in *The Manga Guide to Calculus*. They had just read this section of text on their own during SSR time, but he wants to return to these pages that depict the meeting and initial conversation of Noriko, an aspiring reporter, and Kakeru, the head of a branch office of the *Asagake Times*. Kakeru is explaining to an incredulous Noriko why knowledge of mathematical functions is important in news reporting.

The first request Darnell makes of his students is that they reread those pages. He tells them that complex text does not give up its meaning easily and demands repeated readings. As they reread, Darnell asks that they write in their notes any ideas, questions, or points of confusion. One student writes a question in his notes about why, if function is so important, any letter in addition to f can be used to refer to a function, as Kakeru tells Noriko on the bottom of page 9. Another student writes in her notes that the examples of functions from the newspaper Kakeru shows Noriko remind her of an example from the school cafeteria, how kids' taste for certain foods, such as pizza and grilled cheese sandwiches, are related to how much of certain dishes are left over.

After rereading and taking notes, Darnell tells students to turn to a neighbor and discuss. This approach is consistent with social learning and creating opportunities for his students to develop the ability to question and pose problems as well as communicate with clarity, two important habits of mind. Students talk with their peers about the two pages from the graphic novel with essential information about functions as Darnell walks around the room to listen in on, clarify, and support student conversations. This is an important phase of the close reading process, as it allows students to express their emerging understanding of text and expand their own thinking about text based on their partner's ideas.

Darnell then gains the whole class's attention and asks students to respond to text-dependent questions. These types of questions focus on the text itself, thus requiring evidence from the text to support answers. Darnell's questions about function reinforce close reading by forcing students to return to the graphic novel before answering. The questions are based on his concern that students do not miss important aspects of the text and also come from possible areas of misunderstanding picked up in overhearing student conversations. For example, Darnell asks students, What is the most common way to express a function mathematically? To answer this, students must reread the opening panel at the top of page 9 and Kakeru's speech bubble in which he explains to Noriko that the expression is $y = f(x)$. He also asks what are x and y called, which requires close reading of the bottom large panel on the bottom of page 9 where Kakeru explains that these are called variables. Darnell also invites students to ask their own questions from their notes and conversations with their partners.

Once Darnell is satisfied that his students understand the essential information on those two pages, he expands the level of questioning to explore whether they can see the important relationships in the text and even make applications. One student shares her application about food preferences in the cafeteria and leftovers. As she does, Darnell writes the formulaic relationships on the whiteboard. He asks for others, using the examples Kakeru gives Noriko on page 10 of *The Manga Guide to Calculus*, along with the functional equation.

Darnell's approach to teaching close reading through interactions, modeling, and eliciting as a critical first step to higher levels of thinking builds reading competence and independence (Brozo & Simpson, 2007). This approach also demonstrates for students how, in Darnell's case, a graphic novel can be an engaging read as well as a highly useful information source for learning calculus.

Darnell's philosophy of teaching, encouraging habits of mind and motivating his students to learn math with engaging practices and texts, results in a curriculum that promotes real-world application of newly learned math concepts and processes. Graphic novels like *The Manga Guide to Calculus* are an important aspect of this curriculum. Darnell's approach has many advantages, though principal among them is that it makes the especially complex aspects of math more accessible to his middle-graders, who might otherwise find themselves floundering with more traditional math instruction. Darnell's approach of incorporating graphic novels into his math instruction ensures that all his students are able to participate in meaningful and critical conversations about math, as in functions in calculus. Another major advantage is that for the students who attend Darnell's school, making learning relevant is often the only way to keep them engaged. He knows that bored students can become behavior problems and their skill level can slide lower and lower. Too many youth from the community of Darnell's school have dropped out, leaving them vulnerable to unemployment, gangs, and a galaxy of other personal and financial setbacks. On the other hand, as Darnell's students realize that they can use what they learn in his math class, he reinforces their burgeoning interest by relating what was learned on any particular day to actual careers. For instance, while the class further explores calculus in the graphic novel and other resources, Darnell describes the work of actuaries for insurance companies and financial analysts with brokerage firms.

Probability and Statistics Made Fun with Graphic Novels

Miriam had grown weary of trying to get her 8th-grade math students interested in learning statistics and probability, particularly with the less-than-engaging textbook treatment of the topic. This all changed when she attended a conference workshop and learned about graphic novels that could be used to teach these mathematical processes and principles. With financial help from her principal and school librarian, she was able to purchase multiple copies of three graphic novels for the school math teachers.

One of the books, *The Manga Guide to Statistics* (Takahashi, 2008), is done in classic black-and-white Japanese manga style. Miriam has found that this book can serve as an excellent accompanying or introductory text for her 8th-grade students who are beginning a study of statistics and probability. The book draws readers into an intriguing story in which the heroine, Rui, wants to learn statistics to impress Mr. Igarashi. After begging her father for a tutor, Rui begins her journey into the world of statistics. Her tutor, geeky Mr. Yamamoto, teaches her the basics of statistics, including averages, graphing, and standard deviations, and then delves into the more difficult topics of probability, correlation coefficients, probability distributions, and testing hypotheses. Miriam recognized that the step-by-step calculations offer her students an opportunity to understand more deeply the real meaning of such concepts as variance and standard deviations.

Miriam likes the story because it is engaging and the concepts are applied to real life, such as in test scores, teen magazine quizzes, and games. The exercises and accompanying answer keys are helpful to her students for checking comprehension of the subject matter. Additionally, the appendix shows very clearly how to do all of the major calculations using Microsoft Excel, with Excel spreadsheets available for download from the publisher's website. This feature offers her students the opportunity to practice and apply their newly acquired skills.

Overall, Miriam finds *The Manga Guide to Statistics* easier to read for many of her students than the textbook and its treatment of this difficult topic. The graphic novel's characters make for a very engaging story line that keeps readers interested while presenting difficult content. Furthermore, the technical information is very clearly presented and well integrated into the story line. Finally, even though Miriam knows that many of the detailed formula calculations presented by the authors are highly involved and complex, she believes that exposing her students to these helps to familiarize them with the mathematical processes behind the coefficients, which works to overcome any phobias to statistics they may have.

In the second book Miriam's school purchased, the manga-style *Manga Math Mysteries 8: The Runaway Puppy; A Mystery with Probability* (Barriman & Grutzik, 2011), the authors have woven together with mathematical concepts a story that captures the interest of Miriam's students. In this story, Amy has a surprise for her friends, a new puppy named Brada. Amy named the puppy after one of Charlemagne's knights, Bradamante, because the puppy has golden hair, just like Bradamante. As pups will do, Brada is anxious to play with Amy's friends, and in doing so, manages to scatter all of the leaves that Amy had raked up in the backyard. When Amy and her friends leave, someone leaves the backyard gate unlatched, giving the reader an opportunity to make a prediction about what will happen to Brada.

The kids in the graphic novel all go to the gym for a kung fu class, where they are presented with a question about the probability that each type of gear will be used, learning that probability tells what is likely to happen in the future. They collect data from their available sources and make their prediction. When they return to Amy's house, they use their new skills to predict how long it will take to rake up the scattered leaves. Then the real problem comes to light: Brada has escaped because of the unlatched gate. The challenge for Amy and her friends is to use probability to find the lost puppy.

Miriam finds this story engaging, with good character development. The mystery is well developed and the mathematical principles are integrated effortlessly into the story line. She especially likes that the mathematical concepts are well presented, including the use of clarifying statements and a bar graph to ensure that her students understand the key concepts. The illustrations are also colorful and energetic.

In the third graphic novel Miriam incorporates into her unit on statistics and probability, Gonick and Smith's (1993) *The Cartoon Guide to Statistics*, plenty of wit and humor are used to both illustrate and describe statistical principles, from the most basic to the relatively complex. The range of subjects covered begins with a description of statistics, data, and probability, then delves into the more difficult areas of random variables, distributions, sampling, confidence intervals, hypothesis testing, population comparisons, experimental design, and, finally, regression. Miriam knows that the cartoon format lightens the technical information and terminology the authors present, and ample relevant examples aid her students' understanding. The illustrations are quite humorous, as in the depiction of Roman cartoon figures speaking about probability when playing dice and how it is best to let Caesar win IV out of V.

Along with the descriptions and ample black-and-white illustrations, the graphic novel provides a tour of how modern statistics are useful and how they are utilized in a variety of fields besides the sciences. Miriam's students find the text easy to navigate, especially with a concise table of contents and extensive index. Miriam likes that this graphic novel is appealing to students of differing abilities with statistics, making it a good companion text to help introduce challenging concepts for middle-graders such as probability, sampling, hypothesis testing, and correlations.

After giving short book talks about the three statistics-related graphic novels, Miriam allows students to look through each book to gain a greater appreciation for how they are structured and the abundant content they contain. She skillfully orchestrates the use of the graphic novels to maximize their effectiveness in the unit on statistics. She achieves this by posing a daily big question that necessitates that students use all available resources to conduct research to find an answer. Thus, in addition to the course textbook, other readings, and web-based content, the three graphic novels offer an informative and, for weaker readers and less motivated students, engaging alternative set of resources.

In addition to presenting the daily big question, Miriam creates opportunities for her students to talk about statistical principles and processes and defend their assertions and answers. She is especially concerned about helping students develop a math vernacular that includes using math-specific and academic language reflexively and accurately.

Today, Miriam's class is preparing for a new topic in the statistics unit, hypothesis testing. As always, she begins by directing the class's attention to the interactive whiteboard, where she has written the day's big question: "How can you test the hypothesis that students at our school prefer hot dogs over spaghetti in the cafeteria? Set up a statistical experiment that would test this hypothesis. Be sure to explain your research methods completely and in steps. Also be prepared to defend your methods." She tells them that she will be explaining the hypothesis-testing process, giving examples from everyday life, and that they will read about it in their textbook and the graphic novels. She reminds them that these text sources will be used to help them answer today's big question.

In researching an answer to the day's question, Esmeralda and Latoya first consult the notes they took on Miriam's explanation of hypothesis testing. Miriam gives a formal definition of the concept and also shows how the process could be carried out to find answers to real-world questions. Miriam brings in newspapers to show the class articles that either involved hypothesis-testing directly or to which hypothesis-testing could be applied. For example, she shares a piece about identity theft that includes a quote from a private investigator of identity fraud claiming that people who essentially "live" on the Internet will sooner or later become victims of identity thieves. Miriam then goes to the whiteboard and asks for input from the class to draw out how this assertion or hypothesis could be tested. One suggestion from a student is to interview victims themselves. Miriam refers to the enormous number of people who have their identities stolen every year, making the interview approach impossible. "Not all victims," was the reply, to which Miriam suggests that a representative sample of victims could be interviewed and the results could be statistically applied to all victims of identity theft. This is called probability sampling, she tells her students.

Along with the information and examples from Miriam, Esmeralda and Latoya also consult pages 14 through 22 in *The Manga Guide to Statistics* for additional examples of sampling in order to make an inference about a larger population. The example in the graphic novel focuses on determining if students are interested in reading a book in a series about a fictional high school. Rui's tutor shows her the results of a brief questionnaire of a representative subset of the school's student population who read the book and how these data could be used to decide whether the book is an overall favorite. The two girls also consult the table of contents and index of *The Cartoon Guide to Statistics* and are directed to pages in chapters 6 and 7 that explain the process of taking samples from large populations and making inferences from sample data. Finally, they look through the graph the kids made in an attempt to predict the whereabouts of Amy's lost puppy, Brada, in *The Runaway Puppy: A Mystery with Probability*.

Armed with information from these sources, Esmeralda and Latoya set out to describe how to test their teacher's big question for the day. First, they consider how to gather a representative sample of students from the overall student body at their middle school. They reason that with a total number of 652 kids, they can ask a random sample of 10%, or about 65 kids, about their dietary preferences. Next, they determine that the sampling should be stratified by grade level, 6th, 7th, and 8th. The two then devise a brief questionnaire that not only includes an item about whether a student prefers hot dogs or spaghetti, but also a "neither" option for the student who may be a vegetarian or vegan. Students in these categories who would not prefer either meat lunch choice would get pulled from the sample, they decide.

When students finish their research and write out answers to the big question, Miriam brings students from different pairs together into small groups to engage in "accountable talk to persuade, provide evidence, ask questions of one another, and disagree without being disagreeable" (Frey & Fisher, 2010, p. 32). To support student discussion of their solutions to the statistical problem, Miriam provides them with a framework for making challenges or counter-claims to their peers' ideas and methods, such as (Fisher et al., in press):

- I disagree with _____ because _____.
- The reason I believe _____ is because _____.
- The facts that support my idea are _____.
- One difference between my idea and yours is _____.

After presenting their solutions in the groups, receiving feedback, and making any modifications based on challenges, students then produce a poster that describes each step of their method for testing the hypothesis that students prefer hot dogs over spaghetti in the cafeteria. The posters are stuck to the walls and Miriam invites students to do a gallery walk around the room to analyze the proposals of their peers for testing the hypothesis. Students are given markers and instructed to write constructive questions and comments on the posters.

Finally, Miriam asks selected students to present their solutions and explain in statistical terms the process of testing the hypothesis, including sampling and data analysis procedures. Miriam knows that students will copy from their classmates, but isn't overly concerned about that, since she values the conversations students have with one another, and she can find out what each individual student has learned about statistics on tests and other assignments. What is important is that solving a real-world problem with statistical processes as well as making claims and defending them contribute significantly to student learning.

LOOKING BACK AND MOVING FORWARD

In this chapter we made the case for graphic novels as an invaluable resource for the secondary mathematics teacher. We demonstrated how math graphic novels can not only increase engagement in learning but also serve as an effective tool for instruction and learning.

The three teachers featured in this chapter, Latiffe, Darnell, and Miriam, each knows that for students to learn mathematics at a high level, they need to be catalyzed by engaging texts, content, and practices (Henningsen, 2000; Smith, Bill, & Hughes, 2008). This may be especially critical for disaffected students and those with a history of difficulties learning math content (Lee & Spratley, 2010). And though these teachers recognize that it may be unrealistic to expect all of their students to think like mathematicians, the students can at least work like mathematicians on solving problems that are interesting and meaningful because the problems come from the world around them. Inspiration for application of math principles, concepts, and formulas, as demonstrated in the work of these teachers, can be taken from a wonderful assortment of mathematics-related graphic novels.

Whether it's to enrich the study of the bizarre phenomenon of fractals and then researching authentic careers in this field or to discover applications for calculus and statistics in the everyday lives of youth, graphic novels can be a tool for engaging instruction and source material to inspire student learning.

None of these three teachers described in this chapter or the others featured in the chapters on science, social studies, and English/language arts could have achieved an engaging and responsive curriculum with graphic novels without support. Support in the form of money and resources, planning time, professional development opportunities, and more is essential if teachers are to continue to improve their craft and expand their knowledge.

Study Group Questions for Chapter 6

- What do you and your colleagues see as the biggest challenge to creating a math curriculum at your school that incorporates graphic novels? How can this challenge be overcome?

- Discuss with your colleagues an upcoming math unit. How might graphic novels be used to support student learning in the unit? How could you find potential graphic novels to fit with the content? Work together to research possible graphic novels that could be used in the unit.

- As an individual teacher or teacher team, what strategies can you use to acquire graphic novels for the mathematics program at your school?

- What can your team do to research the effectiveness of graphic novel instruction in the math class? Discuss ways a systematic study of graphic novels could be conducted.

CHAPTER SEVEN

Concluding Thoughts
on Moving Forward

IN THE SIX CHAPTERS OF THIS BOOK, we make the argument that graphic novels can play an important role in the content area curriculum. There can be no doubt that this genre has come into its own, garnering respect for its literary quality and creative art. It is clear that graphic novels are the reading material of choice for many of today's adolescents. In this book, we demonstrate how teachers can combine graphic novels with traditional instructional methods to create engaging lessons. We share lessons that incorporate graphic novels through read-alouds, as whole-class texts, and in cooperative book clubs. And we illustrate how such instruction can align with the Common Core State Standards while addressing traditional themes, goals, and outcomes of education.

You should not view the book as a recipe but rather as a road map to follow. Our intention is to demonstrate the potential for graphic novels in the content classroom. We hope you will think about how you can bring this marvelous resource into your own teaching. We strongly believe that your students will benefit, and you will find your teaching richer, more engaging, and more effective. Based on our own experiences writing this book, we believe that those of you who choose to make the journey into the world of graphic novels will find the trip well worth the effort.

One reason living in the present day is so exciting is the availability and accessibility of information. As graphic novels have evolved into a respected genre, a corresponding explosion has occurred in the availability of both graphic novels and resources related to them. If you choose to take on the task of informing yourself and then staying up to date about graphic novels, your first problem will be to sort through this huge amount of information. As you integrate graphic novels into your teaching, remember that many in the teaching community have confronted the same challenges you may encounter. It is easier than ever to find information that will help you think about what you need to do. In Appendix B, we provide resources to get you started. But more importantly, we encourage you to search on your own: Each journal article we suggest has reference lists with additional resources; each website has links to other websites. Graphic novels have arrived and are widely accepted and respected. Enjoy the journey of informing yourself about this wonderful genre.

So, where do you start? As with any new pedagogical approach, jumping in without purposeful and thoughtful planning can be disastrous. We strongly urge you to mindfully integrate graphic novels into your curriculum. To do this, we encourage you to take some time to explore the genre and discuss the possibilities with colleagues and experts. Here are 11 tips that will help you start your journey.

Tip #1. Read graphic novels for your own enjoyment. There are some excellent adult-level graphic novels now available. A trend we see emerging is graphic novel forms of popular novels. We particularly recommend *The Girl with the Dragon Tattoo, Book 1* (Mina, Mutti, & Manco, 2012) and *Book 2* (2013), and *The Kite Runner Graphic Novel* (Hosseini, 2011). Two other fine adult-level books are *Zahra's Paradise* (Amir & Khalil, 2011), and *Blankets* (Thompson, 2011).

Tip #2. Read graphic novels you think your students would like and will fit into your curriculum. An excellent place to start is Appendix A. We highly recommend *Maus* (Spiegelman, 1986), *Anya's Ghost* (Brosgol, 2011), *Palestine* (Sacco, 2001), *Gettysburg: The Graphic Novel* (Butzer, 2008), *Corpses and Skeletons: The Science of Forensics* (Shone & Spender, 2008), *Chemistry: Getting a Big Reaction* (Green & Basher, 2010), *Prof. E McSquared's Calculus Primer: Expanded Intergalactic Version* (Swann, 1974), and *The Cartoon Guide to Calculus* (Gonick, 2011).

Tip #3. Talk to school and local librarians. This is an important step. You need to enlist the help of your school librarian in developing a robust collection of graphic novels. Both the school and local librarians can provide excellent recommendations of books for you and for your students. And in the event the librarians are not enthusiastic about graphic novels, it is your responsibility to inform them of the importance of this genre.

Tip #4. Talk to students about graphic novels they are reading. This will not only inform you of some of the best new books but will also provide you with information about your students' backgrounds and interests. We often approach adolescents who are reading graphic novels, whether we know them or not, with a question like "What are you reading?" It is a great way to get to know more about middle and high school students.

Tip #5. Discuss the use of graphic novels with colleagues in your department. We expect you'll find both advocates and critics of graphic novels. Hopefully, the advocates will join you in figuring out ways to enhance instruction with graphic novels. Also, you can act as a resource by informing critics of the benefits of their use.

Tip #6. Start a graphic novel book club. One of the best ways to learn about how to read graphic novels is to engage in conversations about the format. As we have pointed out, reading graphic novels is different from reading traditional texts. In addition, book clubs serve to generate interest and enthusiasm about the genre. As a starting point, we recommend you use this book; note that each chapter ends with Study Guide Questions, perfect for a book club.

Tip #7. Review the graphic novel selection at local bookstores. The number and variety may surprise you if you have not looked at the collection of graphic novels in a large bookstore. Even smaller bookstores usually have good selections. Getting to know the manager or acquisitions person may prove useful if you want books ordered for your students.

Tip #8. In this era of mandated curriculum and scripted lessons, get your principal and other administrators on board. Share research to ensure that your supervisors are aware that using graphic novels is pedagogically sound. In the best of situations, your administrators will become advocates. In the worst of situations, shut your classroom door.

Tip #9. Talk with parents about using graphic novels. Your best defense may be your offense. We recommend writing a rationale about how and why graphic novels support and enrich content area learning. Parents need to be on board and can create problems when they are not informed.

Tip #10. Seek outside funding. There is a surprising amount of money available to support teachers engaging in innovative practices. Many organizations require only brief proposals and are easy to manage. A simple Internet search will provide you with many useful websites.

Tip #11. Attend state, national, and international conferences. Conferences sponsored by both the International Reading Association and the National Council of Teachers of English (information is available on their websites) always include sessions on graphic novels. Increasingly, other professional organizations, such as the National Council for the Social Studies, National Council of Teachers of Mathematics, and National Science Teachers Association, are also beginning to address graphic novels at their conferences.

In our careers we have found trends, theories, books, and other conceptual resources that have stimulated our thinking and professional activity. Such resources sometimes come when we seem to be treading water, but they always serve to move us forward in new and interesting directions. We believe that graphic novels may provide the kick start many content teachers are looking for. We hope this book provides inspiration to strive for an innovative approach to your instruction. Our last bit of advice: Start reading!

Graphic Novels by Discipline

English/Language Arts

Backderf, D. (2012). *My friend Dahmer.* New York, NY: Abrams ComicArts.

Brosgol, V. (2011). *Anya's ghost.* New York, NY: First Second.

Burns, C. (2005). *Black hole.* New York, NY: Pantheon.

Butler, N., & Petrus, H. (2010). *Pride and prejudice.* New York, NY: Marvel.

Johnson, M., & Pleece, W. (2009). *Incognegro: A graphic mystery.* New York, NY: Vertigo.

Lloyd, D. (2008). *V for vendetta.* New York, NY: DC Comics.

Long, M., Demonakos, J., & Powell, N. (2012). *The silence of our friends.* New York, NY: First Second.

Miller, F. (1997). *The Dark Knight returns.* New York, NY: DC Comics.

Moore, A., & Gibbons, D. (1995). *Watchmen.* New York, NY: DC Comics.

Moore, A., & O'Neil, K. (2002). *The league of extraordinary gentlemen, Vol. 1.* La Jolla, CA: America's Best Comics.

Thompson, C. (2011). *Blankets.* New York, NY: Top Shelf Productions.

Weaver, L. Q. (2012). *Dark room: A memoir in black and white.* Tuscaloosa, AL: University of Alabama Press.

Yang, G. L. (2008). *American born Chinese.* New York, NY: Square Fish.

History

Abadzis, N. (2007). *Laika.* New York, NY: First Second.

Amir & Khalil. (2011). *Zahra's paradise.* New York, NY: First Second.

Butzer, C. M. (2008). *Gettysburg: The graphic novel.* New York, NY: HarperCollins.

Delisle, G. (2007). *Pyongyang: A journey in North Korea.* Montreal, ON: Draw & Quarterly.

Geary, R. (2008). *J. Edgar Hoover: A graphic biography.* New York, NY: Hill and Wang.

Giardino, V. (1997). *A Jew in communist Prague: A loss of innocence.* Syracuse, NY: Nantier Beall Minoustchine.

Guibert, E. (2008). *Alan's war: The memories of GI Alan Cope.* New York, NY: First Second.

Guibert, E. (2009). *The photographer: Into war-torn Afghanistan with Doctors without Borders.* New York, NY: First Second.

Mills, P. (2005). *Charley's war: Vol. 2. 1 August–17 October, 1916.* London: Titan Books.

Sacco, J. (2001). *Palestine.* Seattle, WA: Fantagraphic Books.

Sacco, J. (2001). *Safe area Gorazde: The war in eastern Bosnia.* Seattle, WA: Fantagraphics Books.

Tan, S. (2006). *The arrival and sketches from a nameless land.* New York, NY: Scholastic.

Tardi, J. (2010). *It was the war of the trenches.* New York, NY: W. W. Norton.

Vaughan, B. K., & Henrichon, N. (2006). *Pride of Baghdad.* New York, NY: Vertigo.

Zinn, H., Buhle, P., & Konopacki, M. (2008). *A people's history of American empire.* New York, NY: Metropolitan Books.

Science

Collicut, P. (2009). *Robot city adventures: Rust attack!* Somerville, MA: Templar Books.

Davis, E. (2009). *The secret science alliance and the copycat crook.* New York, NY: Bloomsbury.

Dingle, A., & Basher, S. (2007). *The periodic table: Elements with style.* Boston, MA: Kingfisher.

Fujitaki, K. (2009). *The manga guide to electricity.* San Francisco, CA: No Starch Press.

Gilpin, D., & Basher, S. (2010). *Planet Earth.* New York, NY: Kingfisher.

Gonick, L., & Criddle, C. (2005). *The cartoon guide to chemistry.* New York, NY: HarperCollins.

Gonick, L., & Outwater, A. (1996). *The cartoon guide to the environment.* New York, NY: HarperCollins.

Green, D., & Basher, S. (2008). *Biology: Life as we know it!* New York, NY: Kingfisher.

Green, D., & Basher, S. (2008). *Physics: Why matter matters!* New York, NY: Kingfisher.

Green, D., & Basher, S. (2010). *Chemistry: Getting a big reaction.* New York, NY: Kingfisher.

Griffith, S., & Bonsen, J. (2007). *Howtoons: The possibilities are endless!* New York, NY: HarperCollins/Regan.

Gonick, L., & Huffman, A. (2005). *The cartoon guide to physics.* New York, NY: Collins Reference.

Gonick, L., & Wheelis, M. (2005). *The cartoon guide to genetics.* New York, NY: Collins Reference.

Hosler, J. (2003). *The sandwalk adventures.* Columbus, OH: Active Synapse.

Hosler, J. (2007). *Clan Apis.* Columbus, OH: Active Synapse.

Hosler, J., Cannon, K., & Cannon, Z. (2011). *Evolution: The story of life on Earth.* New York, NY: Hill & Wang.

Jeffrey, G., & Riley, T. (2008). *Autopsies: Pathologists at work.* New York, NY: Rosen Central.

Keller, M., & Fuller, R. N. (2009). *Charles Darwin's* On the Origin of Species*: A graphic adaptation.* New York, NY: Rodale.

Keyser, A. J., Smith, T. G., & Milgrom, A. (2010). *Decoding genes with Max Axiom, super scientist.* Mankato, MN: Capstone Press.

Krohn, K. (2008). *The 1918 flu pandemic.* Mankato, MN: Capstone Press.

Ottaviani, J. (2001). *Fallout: J. Robert Oppenheimer, Leo Szilard, and the political science of the atomic bomb.* Ann Arbor, MI: G.T. Labs.

Ottaviani, J. (2005). *Bone sharps, cowboys, and thunder lizards: A tale of Edwin Drinker Cope, Othniel Charles Marsh, and the gilded age of paleontology.* Ann Arbor, MI: G.T. Labs.

Phelan, M. (2009). *The storm in the barn.* Somerville, MA: Candlewick Press.

Seidman, D., Whigham, R., & Barnett, C., III. (2007). *Samuel Morse and the telegraph.* Mankato, MN: Capstone Press.

Schultz, M., Cannon, Z., & Cannon, K. (2009). *The stuff of life: A graphic guide to genetics and DNA.* New York, NY: Hill & Wang.

Shiga, J. (2010). *Meanwhile.* New York, NY: Amulet.

Shone, R., & Spender, N. (2008). *Corpses and skeletons: The science of forensics.* New York, NY: Rosen.

Takemura, M. (2009). *The manga guide to molecular biology.* San Francisco, CA: No Starch Press.

Takemura, M. (2011). *The manga guide to biochemistry.* San Francisco, CA: No Starch Press.

Venditti, R., & Weldele, B. (2006). *The surrogates.* Marietta, GA: Top Shelf Productions.

Mathematics

Doxiadis, A., & Papadimitiou, C. (2009). *Logicomix: An epic search for truth.* London: Bloomsbury Press.

Gonick, L. (2011). *The cartoon guide to calculus.* New York, NY: William Morrow Paperbacks.

Green, D. (2010). *Math: A book you can count on.* New York, NY: Kingfisher.

Holm, J. L., & Holm, M. (2009). *Babymouse: Dragonslayer.* New York, NY: Random.

Kojima, H., & Togami, S. (2010). *The manga guide to statistics.* San Francisco, CA: No Starch Press.

Law, F., Way, S., & Spoor, M. (2010). *A storm at sea: Sorting, mapping, and grids in action.* New York, NY: Windmill Books.

Swann, H. (1974). *Prof. E McSquared's calculus primer: Expanded intergalactic version.* Scotts Valley, CA: Dyer and Swann.

Takahasi, S., & Inoue, I. (2012). *The manga guide to linear algebra.* San Francisco, CA: No Starch Press.

Theilbar, M., & Helmer, D. (2010). *The Kung Fu puzzle: A mystery with time and temperature.* New York, NY: Graphic Universe.

Theilbar, M., & Ota, Y. (2009). *The secret ghost: A mystery with distance and measurement.* New York, NY: Graphic Universe.

Theilbar, M., & Pantoja, T. (2010). *The hundred-dollar robber: A mystery with money.* New York, NY: Graphic Universe.

Theilbar, M., & Pantoja, T. (2011). *Manga math mysteries 5: The ancient formula; A mystery with fractions.* New York, NY: Graphic Universe.

Wight, E. (2011). *Frankie Pickle and the mathematical menace.* New York, NY: Simon & Schuster.

Graphic Novel Resources

BOOKS FOR TEACHERS

We found that the single best resource for most information related to graphic novels is librarians. Most librarians, including school, community, and college/university, are well versed in books related to graphic novels and can keep you informed on the newest and most highly regarded resources. Here is a list of five of our favorite books with brief descriptions.

Carter, J. B. (Ed.). (2007). *Building literacy connections with graphic novels: Page by page, panel by panel.* Urbana, IL: National Council of Teachers of English.

> A scholarly effort that covers both theoretical and instructional issues. Examples of how some of the better graphic novels can be adapted for classroom use are provided. Authors of the chapters include many of the most prominent graphic novel scholars.

Gavigan, K., & Tomasevich, M. (2011). *Connecting comics to curriculum: Strategies for grades 6–12.* Santa Barbara, CA: Libraries Unlimited.

> A very pragmatic book, it begins with four chapters that explore issues that must be addressed before graphic novels can be introduced into the classroom. Then, in very practical terms, it shows how they can be integrated into the curriculum. The authors include suggestions and instructional examples of graphic novel use, including motivating students to read, connecting with classical literature, biographies and legends, and writing instruction. There are also chapters that explore the use of graphic novels in content area classes.

Goldsmith, F. (2010). *The readers' advisory guide to graphic novels.* Chicago, IL: American Library Association.

> Provides an excellent orientation for teachers just beginning to use graphic novels. It includes suggestions for encouraging students to become graphic novel readers, a variety of instructional approaches, and a highly useful list of graphic novels organized by genres, topics, and themes.

Gravett. P. (2005). *Graphic novels: Everything you need to know*. New York, NY: Collins Design.

> Panels from 30 of the best currently available graphic novels are showcased in this book. Each chapter begins with a discussion of a literary theme and how graphic novels relate to the theme. Then panels from the 30 graphic novels are explained and used to explore the theme. This is an excellent book for taking a closer and more thoughtful look at the deep literary value of graphic novels.

Kan, K. (2010). *Graphic novels and comic books*. New York, NY: H. W. Wilson.

> Contains a diverse collection of short articles, including scholarly essays, newspaper articles, and online journal and blog entries. It explores the current popularity of graphic novels among adolescents and young adults. Taken together, the articles provide a compelling argument for the literary merit of this genre.

PROFESSIONAL ARTICLES

We present only a limited number of the professional articles that have appeared over the last 2 decades. As with books, there has been a proliferation of articles in the most prestigious journals.

Print

Brozo, W. (2012). Building bridges for boys: Graphic novels in the content classroom. *Journal of Adolescent and Adult Literacy, 55*(6), 550.

> This brief article presents an argument for using graphic novels to engage boys who are struggling or reluctant readers in content area instruction.

Conors, S. P. (2010). "The best of both worlds": Rethinking the literary merits of graphic novels. *ALAN Review, 37*(3), 65–70.

> Develops an argument that graphic novels are not only useful for struggling and reluctant readers but are also a quality genre that deserves attention in its own right. The article traces the history of opposition to comics and graphic novels, acknowledging that many educators continue to be skeptical and resistant to their use. Also explored are secondary students' attitudes.

Hansen, K. S. (2012). In defense of graphic novels. *English Journal, 102*(2), 57–63.

> Examines criticisms of graphic novels and provides justification for their inclusion in the curriculum. Includes an excellent list of mostly online resources as well as suggestions for helping teachers get started using graphic novels.

Hughes, J. M., King, A., Perkins, P., & Fuke, V. (2011) Adolescents and "autographics": Reading and writing coming-of-age graphic novels. *Journal of Adolescent and Adult Literacy, 54*(8), 601–612.

> Discusses how multimodal literacies develop in relation to the use of graphic novels in high school English classes. In two case studies, students who perceived themselves as poor readers first read coming-of-age-graphic novels, then created graphic panels relating personal stories. Examples of the students' work and a discussion of the implications for their literacy learning are included.

MacDonald, H. (2013). How graphic novels became the hottest section in the library. *Publisher's Weekly, 260*(18), 20–25.

> Traces the growth of graphic novels in libraries. Issues related to their acceptance by librarians, teachers, and the adult public are explored.

Schwarz, G. (2006). Expanding literacies through graphic novels. *English Journal, 95*(6), 58–64.

> Provides a coherent argument for including graphic novels in the high school English classroom. Provides specific examples of how graphic novels address English/language arts standards and goals. Also discussed are problems teachers can expect to face when first implementing graphic novels in their instruction.

Online

The National Coalition against Censorship. (2006). *Graphic novels: Suggestions for librarians.* Available at www.ala.org/offices/sites/ala.org.offices/files/content/oif/ifissues/graphicnovels _1.pdf

> A joint publication of the National Coalition against Censorship, the American Library Association, and the Comic Book Legal Defense Fund, this article provides suggestions and resources for building library holdings of graphic novels.

National Council of Teachers of English. (2005). *Using comics and graphic novels in the classroom.* Available at www.ncte.org/magazine/archives/122031

> A brief overview of steps to take when using graphic novels in language arts instruction.

Scholastic Inc. (2013). *Using graphic novels with children and teens: A guide for teachers and librarians.* Available at www.scholastic.com/teachers/lesson-plan/using-graphic-novels -children-and-teens-guide-teachers-and-librarians

> A commercial publication from Scholastic Inc., this provides implementation guidelines, including a good list of resources.

Shanower, E. (2004). *The art of the graphic novel.* Available at www.scholar.lib.vt.edu/ ejournals/ALAN/v32n2/shanower.pdf

> Examines graphic novels as an art form.

WEBSITES

The number of websites devoted to graphic novels and comic books is staggering and growing. We urge you to familiarize yourself with the websites of three professional organizations that advocate the use of graphic novels in education: the American Library Association (ALA), the International Reading Association (IRA), and the National Council of Teachers of English (NCTE). In addition, the IRA and NCTE cosponsor the ReadWriteThink (RWT) website, a collection of teacher-developed lessons. Here are brief overviews of each organization's websites and resources related to graphic novels.

ALA (www.ala.org/). Includes many helpful resources, including extensive lists of quality graphic novels (www.ala.org/yalsa/great-graphic-novels), online classes and webinars, and online articles.

IRA (www.reading.org/). The strength of this website is its resources for adolescent literacy instruction, including instruction in the content areas. Of special interest are the annual best book awards, as chosen both by teachers (www.reading.org/Resources/Booklists/TeachersChoices.aspx) and young adults (www.reading.org/Resources/Booklists/YoungAdultsChoices.aspx).

NCTE (www.ncte.org/). The website includes excellent sections for secondary (www.ncte.org/second) and middle (www.ncte.org/middle) school teachers.

RWT (www.readwritethink.org/). Provides over 30 middle and high school lesson plans built around graphic novels as well as other resources, including podcasts, journal articles, and instructional activities. Search "graphic novels" on the main page for a complete listing.

Additional Websites

Here are a few additional websites we've found particularly useful for suggestions for quality graphic novels. Once you begin using these, you will find it easy to find additional resources.

Graphic Novels for Teens (Internet Public Library): www.ipl.org/div/graphicnovels/

Graphic Novels and High School English: www.graphicnovelsandhighschoolenglish.com/

Goodreads Choice Awards for 2012: www.goodreads.com/choiceawards/best-graphic-novels-comics-2012#74597-Best-Graphic-Novels-&-Comics

Goodreads Graphic Novels: www.goodreads.com/genres/graphic-novels

Greatest Graphic Novels of All Time: www.amazon.com/Greatest-Graphic-Novels-all-Time/lm/RYC07UF1DW4JP

The Best Comics and Graphic Novels of the Decade 2000-2009

www.amazon.com/Comics-Graphic-Novels-Decade-2000-2009/lm/R2FE9OTUO88SAW

Forbidden Planet 50 Best of the Best Graphic Novels: www.forbiddenplanet.com/picks
/50-best-graphic-novels/

Fifty best graphic novels of all times according to Glen R. Downey: www.pinterest.com/
glenrdowney/the-best-graphic-novels-of-all-time/

Best Graphic Novels: History

www.goodreads.com/list/show/8998.History_through_graphic_novels

www.amazon.com/Historical-Graphic-Novels/lm/R1XZF2TFVGIMXZ

Best Graphic Novels: Science and Math

From the Science Library at Pennsylvania State University: www.personal.psu.edu/jjm38
/sciencegraphicnovels.pdf

Timberdoodle: www.timberdoodle.com/Graphic_Novels_Science_s/354.htm

Booklist Online

www.booklistonline.com/Classroom-Connections-Graphic-Novels-with-Science-and-
Math-Themes-Ian-Chipman/pid=4268442

Graphic Lessons and CCSS

We believe graphic novels and comics can successfully align with any set of standards and be integrated into any curriculum. In order to demonstrate how the thoughtful use of graphic novels can help teachers meet the standards they are asked to use, we provide the following charts. The charts illustrate how the graphic novels and the corresponding activities can scaffold student learning and help students to meet the standards outlined in the CCSS. For example, when Kathy asks her students to read the graphic version of the 9/11 report, and complete two-column notes, Kathy has implemented an activity that will help her students meet reading standards 1, 2, 6, 7, and 10. In addition, the 9/11 activities will help students meet writing standards 2, 4, 9, and 10.

English/Language Arts College and Career Readiness Anchor Standards for Reading

ACTIVITIES	Key Idea Detail			Craft and Structure			Integration of Knowledge and Ideas			Range of Reading and Text Complexity
	1	2	3	4	5	6	7	8	9	10
Reading *Beowulf* paired with Think-Pair-Share	X	X	X	X			X			X
Reading, viewing, and performing *Romeo and Juliet*	X	X		X		X	X		X	X
Graphic novel book clubs and literary themes	X	X	X		X		X		X	X

English/Language Arts College and Career Readiness Anchor Standards for Writing

ACTIVITIES	Text Types and Purposes			Production and Distribution of Writing			Research to Build and Present Knowledge			Range of Writing
	1	2	3	4	5	6	7	8	9	10
Reading *Beowulf* paired with Think-Pair-Share	X	X								X
Reading, viewing, and performing *Romeo and Juliet*					n/a					
Graphic novel book clubs and literary themes	X	X	X	X		X			X	X

History/Social Studies College and Career Readiness Anchor Standards for Reading

ACTIVITIES	Key Idea Detail			Craft and Structure			Integration of Knowledge and Ideas			Range of Reading and Text Complexity
	1	2	3	4	5	6	7	8	9	10
Reading *300* paired with Socratic Seminar	X	X	X	X			X			X
Reading *9/11 Report* with two-column notes	X	X				X	X			X
Book clubs paired with online discussion	X	X	X				X		X	X

History/Social Studies College and Career Readiness Anchor Standards for Writing

ACTIVITIES	Text Types and Purposes			Production and Distribution of Writing			Research to Build and Present Knowledge			Range of Writing
	1	2	3	4	5	6	7	8	9	10
Reading *300* paired with Socratic Seminar					n/a					
Reading *9/11 Report* with two-column notes		X		X					X	X
Book clubs paired with online discussion	X					X	X	X	X	X

Science College and Career Readiness Anchor Standards for Reading

ACTIVITIES	Key Idea Detail			Craft and Structure			Integration of Knowledge and Ideas			Range of Reading and Text Complexity
	1	2	3	4	5	6	7	8	9	10
Read-aloud: *Genome* paired with SPAWN	X	X		X			X			X
Going to the moon with *T-Minus*: Middle-grades science	X			X			X			X
Introduction to physics with multiple graphic novels	X			X	X		X		X	X

Science College and Career Readiness Anchor Standards for Writing

ACTIVITIES	Text Types and Purposes			Production and Distribution of Writing			Research to Build and Present Knowledge			Range of Writing
	1	2	3	4	5	6	7	8	9	10
Read-aloud: *Genome* paired with SPAWN		X		X				X	X	X
Going to the moon with *T-Minus*: Middle-grades science		X		X		X		X	X	X
Introduction to physics with multiple graphic novels		X		X				X	X	X

Technical Subjects College and Career Readiness Anchor Standards for Reading

ACTIVITIES	Key Idea Detail			Craft and Structure			Integration of Knowledge and Ideas			Range of Reading and Text Complexity
	1	2	3	4	5	6	7	8	9	10
Exploring the strange world of fractals in high school geometry	X	X	X	X			X		X	X
An introduction to calculus with manga	X	X		X			X		X	X
Probability and statistics made fun with graphic novels	X	X		X	X	X	X	X	X	X

Technical Subjects College and Career Readiness Anchor Standards for Writing

ACTIVITIES	Text Types and Purposes			Production and Distribution of Writing			Research to Build and Present Knowledge			Range of Writing
	1	2	3	4	5	6	7	8	9	10
Exploring the strange world of fractals in high school geometry	X	X		X				X	X	X
An introduction to calculus with manga				X						X
Probability and statistics made fun with graphic novels	X	X		X	X	X	X	X	X	X

References

GRAPHIC NOVELS CITED IN TEXT

Amir & Khalil. (2011). *Zahra's paradise*. New York, NY: First Second.

Appignanesi, R., & Mustashrik, M. (2008). *Julius Caesar*. New York, NY: Amulet Books.

Barriman, L., & Grutzik, B. (2011). *Manga math mysteries 8: The runaway puppy; A mystery with probability*. New York, NY: Graphic Universe.

Bassett. B., & Edney, R. (2005). *Introducing relativity: A graphic guide*. Thriplow, Cambridge, UK: Icon Books.

Biskup, A. (2011). *The dynamic world of chemical reactions with Max Axiom*. North Mankato, MN: Capstone Press.

Bowen, R., & Garcia, E. (2012). *Julius Caesar*. Basingstoke Hants, UK: Raintree Paperbacks.

Boyd, B. (2003). *Slavery's storm*. Williamsburg, VA: Chester Comix.

Brosgol, V. (2011). *Anya's ghost*. New York, NY: First Second.

Butzer, C. M. (2008). *Gettysburg: The graphic novel*. New York, NY: HarperCollins.

Eisner, W. (2006). *A contract with God and other tenement stories*. New York, NY: W. W. Norton.

Fetter-Vorm, J. (2012). *Trinity: A graphic history of the first atomic bomb*. New York, NY: Hill and Wang.

Feynman, R., Leighton, R., Hutchings, E., & Hibbs, A. (1997). *Surely you're joking, Mr. Feynman! (Adventures of a curious character)*. New York, NY: W. W. Norton.

Geary, R. (2005). *The murder of Abraham Lincoln*. New York, NY: NBM Publishing.

Glasgow, A. D., & Schichtel, JM. (n.d.). *Genome: The graphic novel*. Seattle, WA: Amazon.

Gonick, L. (2011). *The cartoon guide to calculus*. New York, NY: William Morrow Paperbacks.

Gonick, L., & Smith, W. (1993). *The cartoon guide to statistics*. New York, NY: HarperCollins.

Green, D., & Basher, S. (2010). *Chemistry: Getting a big reaction*. New York, NY: Kingfisher.

Hama, L., & Williams, A. (2006a). *The bloodiest day: Battle of Antietam*. New York, NY: Random.

Hama, L,. & Williams, A. (2006b). *Island of terror: Battle of Iwo Jima*. Oxford, UK: Osprey.

Helfand, L., & Manikandan. (2012). *Abraham Lincoln: From the log cabin to the White House* [Campfire heroes line]. Sherman Oaks, CA: Campfire.

Hinds, G. (2007). *Beowulf*. Cambridge, MA: Candlewick Press.

Hosseini, K. (2011). *The kite runner graphic novel*. New York, NY: Riverhead Trade.

Jablonski, C., & Purvis, L. (2007). *Resistance, Book 1*. New York, NY: First Second.

Jacobson, S., & Colón, E. (2006). *The 9/11 Report: A graphic adaptation*. New York, NY: Hill and Wang.

Jacobson, S., & Colón, E. (2010). *Anne Frank: The Anne Frank House authorized graphic biography*. New York, NY: Hill and Wang.

Jerwa, B., Trautmann, E., & Lieber, S. (2012). *Shooters*. New York, NY: Vertigo.

Johnson, M., & Pleece, W. (2009). *Incognegro*. London: Titan Books.

Keyser, A. J., Smith, T. G., & Milgrom, A. (2010). *Decoding genes with Max Axiom, super scientist*. Mankato, MN: Capstone Press.

Kojima, H., & Togami, S. (2010). *The manga guide to calculus*. San Francisco, CA: No Starch Press.

Lesmoir-Gordon, N., Rood, W., & Edney, R. (2009). *Introducing fractals: A graphic guide*. Thriplow, Cambridge, UK.: Icon Books.

Love, J. (2009). *Bayou, volume 1*. New York, NY: DC Comics.

Martin, M., & Anderson, B. (2005). *Harriet Tubman and the Underground Railroad*. Mankato, MN: Capstone.

McDonald, J., & Shakespeare, W. (2009). *Romeo and Juliet, the graphic novel: Original text*. Towecester, UK: Classic Comics LTD.

Miller, F., & Varley, L. (1999). *300*. Milwaukie, OR: Dark House Books.

Mina, D., Mutti, A., & Manco, L. (2012). *The girl with the dragon tattoo, book 1 (Millennium trilogy)*. New York, NY: Vertigo.

Mina, D., Mutti, A., & Manco, L. (2013). *The girl with the dragon tattoo, book 2 (Millennium trilogy)*. New York, NY: Vertigo.

Murphy, J. (2008). *Cleburne: A graphic novel*. Rampart Press.

Murray, D. (1987). *'Nam*. New York, NY: Marvel.

Murray, D., & Williams, A. (2007). *The tide turns: D-Day invasion*. Oxford, UK: Osprey.

Neri, G. (2010). *Yummy: The last days of a southside shorty*. New York, NY: Lee & Low Books.

Neufeld, J. (2010). *A.D.: New Orleans after the deluge*. New York, NY: Pantheon Books.

Nitta, H., & Takatsu, K. (2010). *The manga guide to physics*. San Francisco, CA: No Starch Press.

Ottaviani, J. (2006). *Suspended in language: Niels Bohr's life, discoveries, and the century he shaped*. Ann Arbor, MI: G.T. Labs.

Ottavani, J., Cannon, Z., & Cannon, K. (2009). *T-Minus: The race to the moon*. New York, NY: Aladdin.

Ottaviani, J., & Myrick, L. (2011). *Feynman*. New York, NY: Roaring Brook Press.

Sacco, J. (2001). *Palestine*. Seattle, WA: Fantagraphic Books.

Schultz, M., Cannon, Z., & Cannon, K. (2009). *The stuff of life: A graphic guide to genetics and DNA*. New York, NY: Hill & Wang.

Shone, R., & Spender, N. (2008). *Corpses and skeletons: The science of forensics*. New York, NY: Rosen.

Spiegelman, A. (1986). *Maus: A survivor's tale*. New York, NY: Pantheon Books.

Swann, H. (1974). *Prof. E McSquared's calculus primer: Expanded intergalactic version*. Scotts Valley, CA: Dyer and Swann.

Takahashi, S. (2008). *The manga guide to statistics*. San Francisco, CA: No Starch Press.

Theilbar, M., & Pantoja, T. (2011). *Manga math mysteries 5: The ancient formula; A mystery with fractions*. New York, NY: Graphic Universe.

Thompson, C. (2011). *Blankets*. Marietta, GA: Top Shelf Productions.

Yamamoto, M., Takatsu, K., & Nitta, H. (2011). *The manga guide to relativity*. San Francisco, CA: No Starch Press.

Zimmerman, D., & Vansant, W. (2012). *The hammer and the anvil: Frederick Douglass, Abraham Lincoln, and the end of slavery in America*. New York, NY: Hill and Wang.

GENERAL REFERENCES

Albright, L. K. (2002). Bringing the ice maiden to life: Engaging adolescents in learning through picture book read-alouds in the content area. *Journal of Adolescent and Adult Literacy, 45,* 418–428.

Albright, L. K., & Ariail, M. (2005). Tapping the potential of teacher read-alouds in middle schools. *Journal of Adolescent & Adult Literacy, 48,* 582–591.

Alexander, P. (2007, July). What's love got to do with it? The role of motivation in strategic learning and strategic teaching. Paper presented at the Strategic Instruction Model international conference, University of Kansas, Lawrence, KS.

Alvermann, D. E. (2002). Effective literacy instruction for adolescents. *Journal of Literacy Research, 34,* 189–208.

Anderson, R. C., & Pearson, P. D. (1984). A schema-theoretic view of basic processes in reading comprehension. *Handbook of Reading Research, 1,* 255–291.

Ausman, B. D., Lin, H., Kidwai, K., Munyofu, M., Swain, W. J., & Dwyer, F. (2004). *Effects of varied animation strategies in facilitating animated instruction*. Chicago: Association for Educational Communications and Technology. (ERIC Document No. ED484987)

Bakis, M. (2013). Why I teach comics in secondary education. *Knowledge Quest, 41*(3), 66–67.

Baumann, J. F. (1992). Commentary: Basal reading programs and the deskilling of teachers: A critical examination of the argument. *Reading Research Quarterly, 27,* 390–398.

Beck, I., & McKeown, M. (1991). Research directions: Social studies texts are hard to understand—mediating some of the difficulties. *Language Arts, 68,* 482–490

Beck, I., McKeown, M., & Worthy, J. (1995). Giving text a voice can improve students' understanding. *Reading Research Quarterly, 30,* 220–238.

Bill, V. L., & Jamar, I. (2010). Disciplinary literacy in the mathematics classroom. In S. McConachie & A. Petrosky (Eds.), *Content matters: A disciplinary literacy approach to improving student learning* (pp. 63–87). San Francisco: Jossey-Bass.

Blum, H. T., Lipsett, L. R., & Yocom, D. J. (2002). Literature circles: A tool for self-determination in one middle school inclusive classroom. *Remedial and Special Education, 23,* 99–108.

Boerman-Cornell, W. (2010). History is relatives: Educational affordances of the graphic novel in the magical life of Long Tack Sam. *International Journal of Comic Art, 12,* 147–156.

Botzakis, S. (2009). Adult fans of comic books: What they get out of reading. *Journal of Adolescent and Adult Literacy, 53*(1), 50–59.

Botzakis, S. (2011). "To be a part of the dialog": American adults reading comic books. *Journal of Graphic Novels and Comics, 2,* 113–123.

Boyles, N. (2012/2013). Closing in on close reading. *Educational Leadership, 70*(4), 36–41.

Brown, B. (2001). Pairing William Faulkner's *Light in August* and Art Spiegelman's *Maus.* In A. Ruggles Gere & P. Shaheen (Eds.), *Classroom practices in teaching English* (pp. 148–155). Urbana, IL: National Council of Teachers of English.

Brozo, W. G. (2005). Book review: *Adolescents and Literacies in a Digital World. Journal of Literacy Research, 36*(4), 533–538.

Brozo, W. G. (2010). *To be a boy, to be a reader: Engaging teen and preteen boys in active literacy.* Newark, DE: International Reading Association.

Brozo, W. G., Moorman, G., Meyer, C. K., & Stewart, T. T. (2013). Content area reading and disciplinary literacy: A case for the radical center. *Journal of Adolescent and Adult Literacy, 56,* 353–357.

Brozo, W. G., & Simpson, M. L. (2007). *Content literacy for today's adolescents: Honoring diversity and building competence.* Upper Saddle River, NJ: Pearson.

Brozo, W. G., & Tomlinson, C. M. (1986). Literature: The key to lively content courses. *The Reading Teacher, 40,* 288–293.

Carrier, K. A. (2005). Supporting science learning through science literacy objectives for English language learners. *Science Activities: Classroom Projects and Curriculum Ideas, 42*(2), 5.

Carter, J. B. (2007). *Building literacy connections with graphic novels: Page by page, panel by panel.* Urbana, IL: National Council of Teachers of English.

Carter, J. B. (2009, March). Going graphic. *Educational Leadership, 66*(6), 68–72.

Cheesman, K. (2006). Using comics in the science classroom: A pedagogical tool. *Journal of College Science Teaching, 35*(4), 48–51.

Chun, C. W. (2009). Critical literacies and graphic novels for English language learners: Teaching *Maus. Journal of Adolescent and Adult Literacy, 53,* 144–153.

Clarke, J. H., & Agne, R. M. (1997). *Interdisciplinary high school teaching: Strategies for integrated learning.* Boston, MA: Allyn and Bacon.

Cohen, L. S. (2013). But this book has pictures! The case for graphic novels in the AP classroom. *AP Central.* Available at www.apcentral.collegeboard.com/apc/members/courses/teachers_corner/158535.html

Collier, L. (2007, November). The shift to 21st-century literacies. *The Council Chronicle, 17*(2), 4–8.

Considine, D., Horton, J., & Moorman, G. (2009). Teaching and reaching the millennial generation through media literacy. *Journal of Adolescent and Adult Literacy, 52,* 471–481.

Cope, B., & Kalantzis, M. (2000). *Multiliteracies: Literacy learning and the design of social futures.* London, UK: Routledge.

Costa, A. L., & Kallick, B. (2000). *Activating and engaging habits of mind.* Alexandria, VA: Association for Supervision and Curriculum Development.

Coville, J. (2013). *Seduction of the innocents and the attack on comic books.* Available at www.psu .edu/dept/inart10_110/inart10/cmbk4cca.html

Cromer, M., & Clark, P. (2007). Getting graphic with the past: Graphic novels and the teaching of history. *Theory and Research in Social Education, 35*(4), 574–591.

Daniels, H. (2002). Resources for middle school book clubs. *Voices from the Middle, 10,* 48–49.

Darling-Hammond, L. (1997). *Doing what matters most: Investing in quality teaching.* New York, NY: National Commission on Teaching and America's Future.

Davis, M., & Hobson, M. (Writers) & Jersey, B., & Schwartz, M. (Directors). (2008). Hunting the hidden dimension. In D. J. Roller (Producer), *Nova.* Arlington, VA: PBS.

Derry, S. J., Schunn, C. D., & Gernsbacher, M. A. (2005). *Interdisciplinary collaboration: An emerging cognitive science.* Mahwah, NJ: Erlbaum.

Dewdney, A. K. (1984). *The planiverse.* New York, NY: Poseidon Press.

Dewdney, A. K. (2000). The planiverse project: Then and now. *The Mathematical Intelligencer, 22,* 46–51.

Donohoo, J. (2010). Learning how to learn: Cornell notes as an example. *Journal of Adolescent and Adult Literacy, 54,* 224–227.

Dowdy, J. K. (2002). Ovuh Dyuh. In L. Delpit & J. K. Dowdy (Eds.), *The skin that we speak: Thoughts on language and culture in the classroom* (pp. 3–13). New York, NY: The New Press.

Dredger, K., Woods, D., Beach, C., & Sagstetter, V. (2010). Engage me: Using new literacies to create third space classrooms that engage student writers. *Journal of Media Literacy Education, 2*(2), 85–101.

Dreher, S. (2003). A novel idea: Reading aloud in a high school English classroom. *English Journal, 93,* 50–53.

Duffy, D. (2010). Out of the margins . . . into the panels: Toward a theory of comics as a medium of critical pedagogy in library instruction. In M. T. Accardi, E. Drabinski, & A. Kumbier (Eds.), *Critical library instruction: Theories and methods* (pp. 199–219). Duluth, MN: Library Juice Press

Eisner, W. (2008). *Comics and sequential art: Principles and practices from a legendary cartoonist.* New York, NY: W. W. Norton.

EMC. (2005). *English and the language arts: Experiencing literature.* St Paul, MN: EMC/Paradigm.

Faggella-Luby, M. N., Graner, P. S., Deshler, D. D., & Drew, S. V. (2012). Building a house on sand: Why disciplinary literacy is not sufficient to replace general strategies for adolescent learners who struggle. *Topics in Language Disorders, 32*(1), 69–84.

Fang, Z. (2006). The language demands of science reading in middle school. *International Journal of Science Education, 28,* 491–520.

Fisher, D., Brozo, W. G., Frey, N., & Ivey, G. (in press). *50 instructional routines to develop content literacy* (3rd ed.). New York, NY: Pearson.

Fisher, D., Brozo, W. G., Frey, N., & Ivey, G. (2011). *50 instructional routines to develop content literacy* (2nd ed.). New York, NY: Pearson.

Fisher, D., & Frey, N. (2008). *Better learning through structured teaching: A framework for the gradual release of responsibility.* Alexandria, VA: Association for Supervision and Curriculum Development.

Fisher, D., Frey, N., & Lapp, D. (2011). Coaching middle-level teachers to think aloud improves comprehension instruction and reading achievement. *The Teacher Educator, 46,* 231–243.

Fisher, D., Frey, N., & Lapp, D. (2012). *Text complexity: Raising rigor in reading.* Newark, DE: International Reading Association.

Fisher, D., Zike, D., & Frey, N. (2007, August). Foldables: Improving learning with 3-D interactive graphic organizers. *Classroom Notes Plus, 25*(1), 1–12.

Francois, C. (2013). Reading in the crawl space: A study of an urban school's literacy-focused community of practice. *Teachers College Record, 115*(5), 1–35.

Freire, P. (1970). *Pedagogy of the oppressed.* New York, NY: Herder and Herder.

Freire, P., & Macedo, D. (1987). *Literacy: Reading the word and the world.* London: Routledge and Kegan Paul.

Frey, N., & Fisher, D. (2010). Motivation requires a meaningful task. *English Journal, 100*(1), 30–36.

Garan, E. M., & DeVoogd, G. (2008). The benefits of Sustained Silent Reading: Scientific research and common sense converge. *The Reading Teacher, 62*(4), 336–344.

Gardiner, S. (2005). *Building student literacy through Sustained Silent Reading.* Alexandria, VA: Association for Supervision and Curriculum Development.

Gavigan, K. W. (2010). Examining struggling male adolescent readers' responses to graphic novels: A multiple case study of four, eighth-grade males in a graphic novel book club. Available at Dissertations and Theses database (AAT3418818).

Goodlad, J. (1984). *A place called school.* New York, NY: McGraw-Hill.

Goodman, S. (2003). *Teaching youth media: A critical guide to literacy, video production, and social change.* New York, NY: Teachers College Press.

Goos, M. (2004). Learning mathematics in a classroom community of inquiry. *Journal for Research in Mathematics Education, 35,* 258–291.

Gorman, M. (2003). *Getting graphic! Using graphic novels to promote literacy with preteens and teens.* Worthington, OH: Linworth.

Gravett, P. (2005). *Graphic novels: Everything you need to know.* New York, NY: Collins Design.

Grisham, D. L., & Wolsey, T. D. (2006). Recentering the middle school classroom as a vibrant learning community: Students, literacy, and technology intersect. *Journal of Adult and Adolescent Literacy, 49,* 648–660.

Guthrie, J. (2007). *Engaging adolescents in reading.* Thousand Oaks, CA: Corwin Press.

Guthrie, J., & Wigfield, A. (2000). Engagement and motivation in reading. In M. Kamil, P. Mosenthal, P. D. Pearson, & R. Barr (Eds.), *Handbook of reading research* (Vol. 3, 403–422). Mahwah, NJ: Lawrence Erlbaum Associates.

Hajdu, D. (2004, September 12). Homeland insecurity [Review of the book *In the shadow of no towers*]. *The New York Times.* Available at www.nytimes.com/2004/09/12/books/review/12HAJDU.html?_r=0

Halimun, J. M. (2011). A qualitative study of the use of content-related comics to promote student participation in mathematical discourse in a math I support class. *Dissertations, Theses and Capstone Projects* (Paper 471). Available at www.digitalcommons.kennesaw.edu/etd/471

Halpern, C. M., & Halpern, P. A. (2005–2006). Using creative writing and literature in mathematics class. *Mathematics Teaching in the Middle School, 11,* 226–230.

Hancock, D. (2004). Cooperative learning and peer orientation effects on motivation and achievement. *The Journal of Educational Research, 97*(3), 159–166.

Hand, B. M., Prain, V., & Yore, L. D. (2001). Sequential writing tasks' influence on science learning. In P. Tynjala, L. Mason, & K. Lonka (Eds.), *Writing as a learning tool: Integrating theory and practice* (pp. 105–129). Dordrecht, The Netherlands: Kluwer.

Hansen, K. (2012). In defense of graphic novels. *English Journal, 102,* 57–63.

Hapgood, S., & Palincsar, A. S. (2007). Where literacy and science intersect. *Educational Leadership, 64*(4), 56–60.

Henningsen, M. A. (2000). Engaging middle school students with cognitively challenging mathematical tasks: Classroom factors that influence students' high-level thinking, reasoning, and communication during consecutive lessons. Unpublished doctoral dissertation. University of Pittsburgh.

Hill, B. C., Noe, K. L., & King, J. A. (2003). *Literature circles in middle school: One teacher's journey.* Norwood, MA: Christopher-Gordon.

Ho, F. F., & Boo, H. K. (2007). Cooperative learning: Exploring its effectiveness in the physics classroom. *Asia-Pacific Forum on Science Learning and Teaching, 8*(2). Available at www.ied.edu.hk/apfslt/v8_issue2/hoff/index.htm

Holt, Rinehart and Winston. (2006). *Elements of literature: First course.* Austin, TX: Author.

Hosler, J. (2007). Comic book science. *Juniata Voices, 7,* 1–9.

Inge, M. T. (1990). *Comics as culture.* Jackson, MS: University Press of Mississippi.

Jetton, T. L., & Alexander, P. A. (2004). Domains, teaching, and literacy. In T. L. Jetton & J. A. Dole (Eds.), *Adolescent literacy research and practice* (pp. 15–36). New York, NY: Guilford Press.

Jetton, T. L., & Dole, J. A. (Eds.). (2004). *Adolescent literacy research and practice.* New York, NY: Guilford.

Kabapınar, F. (2005). Effectiveness of teaching via concept cartoons from the point of view of constructivist approach. *Educational Sciences: Theory and Practice, 5,* 135–146.

Kajder, S. (2010). *Adolescents and digital literacies: Learning alongside our students.* Urbana, IL: National Council of Teachers of English.

Kan, K. (2010). *Graphic novels and comic books.* New York, NY: H. W. Wilson.

Kerr, S., & Culhane, T. H. (2000, July). The humble comic: Possibilities for developing literacy skills and learning content. Available at www.pearsonlearning.com/correlation/rsp/ResearchPaper_Comic.pdf

Kessler, B. (2009). Comic books that teach mathematics. *2009 Bridges Banff Conference Proceedings*. Available at www.digitalcommons.wku.edu/math_fac_pub/10

Knain, E. (2006). Achieving science literacy through transformation of multimodal textual resources. *Science Education, 90,* 656–659.

Kraft, N. P. (1995). The dilemmas of deskilling: Reflections of a staff developer. *Journal of Staff Development, 27,* 390–398.

Krashen, S. D. (2004). *The power of reading: Insights from the research* (2nd ed.). Westport, CT: Libraries Unlimited.

Kress, G., & Van Leeuwen, T. (2001). *Multimodal discourse: The modes and media of contemporary communication.* New York, NY: Oxford University Press.

Lankshear, C., & Knobel, M. (2002). Do we have your attention? New literacies, digital technologies, and the education of adolescents. In D. Alvermann (Ed.), *Adolescents and literacies in a digital world* (pp. 19–39). New York: Peter Lang.

Latendresse, C. (2004). Literature circles: Meeting reading standards, making personal connections, and appreciating others' interpretations. *Middle School Journal, 35*(3), 13–20.

Lee, C. D. (1997). Bridging home and school literacies: Models for culturally responsive teaching, a case for African American English. In J. Flood, S. B. Heath, & D. Lapp (Eds.), *Handbook of research on teaching literacy through the communicative and visual arts* (pp. 334–345). New York, NY: Macmillan.

Lee, C. D., & Spratley, A. (2010). *Reading in the disciplines: The challenge of adolescent literacy.* New York, NY: Carnegie Corporation of New York.

Lent, R. C., & Pipkin, G. (2013). *Keep them reading: An anti-censorship handbook for educators.* New York, NY: Teachers College Press.

Luhrmann, B. (Director), & Martinelli, G. (Producer). (1996). *William's Shakespeare's Romeo + Juliet* [Motion Picture]. United States: 20th Century Fox.

Lydersen, K., & Ortiz, C. J. (2012). More young people are killed in Chicago than any other American city. Available at www.chicagoreporter.com/news/2012/01/more-young-people-are-killed-chicago-any-other-american-city

MacDonald, H. (2013). How graphic novels became the hottest section in the library. *Publishers Weekly, 260*(18), 20–25.

Mackey, M., & McClay, J. K. (2000). Graphic routes to electronic literacy: Polysemy and picture books. *Changing English, 7*(2), 191–201.

Martin, C., Martin, M., & O'Brien, D. (1984). Spawning ideas for writing in the content areas. *Reading World, 11,* 11–15.

McCabe, P. P. (1993). Considerateness of fifth-grade social studies texts. *Theory and Research in Social Education, 21,* 128–142.

McCloud, S. (1994). *Understanding comics: The invisible art.* New York, NY: William Marrow.

McPhail, J., Pierson, J., & Freeman, J. (2000). The role of interest in fostering sixth grade students' identities as competent learners. *Curriculum Inquiry, 30*(1), 43–70.

McTaggert, J. (2005). Using comics and graphic novels to encourage reluctant readers. *Reading Today, 23*(2), 46.

Moje, E. B., McIntosh Ciechanowski, K., Kramer, K., Ellis, L., Carrillo, R., & Collazo, T. (2004). Working toward third space in content area literacy: An examination of everyday funds of knowledge and discourse. *Reading Research Quarterly, 39*, 38–70.

Monnin, K. (2010). *Teaching graphic novels: Practical strategies for the secondary ELA classroom.* Gainesville, FL: Maupin House.

Mooney, M. (2002). Graphic novels: How they can work in libraries. *The Book Report, 21*, 18–19.

Moorman, G., & Horton, J. (2007). *Millennials and how to teach them.* In J. Lewis & G. Moorman (Eds.), *Adolescent literacy instruction: Policies and promising practice.* Newark, DE: International Reading Association.

Morrison, T. G., Bryan, G., & Chilcoat, G. W. (2002). Using student-generated comic books in the classroom. *Journal of Adolescent and Adult Literacy, 45*, 758–767.

Mullis, I. V. S., Martin, M. O., Foy, P., & Arora, A. (2011). *TIMSS 2011 international results in mathematics.* Boston, MA: TIMSS & PIRLS International Study Center.

Musoleno, R. R., & White, G. P. (2010). Influences of high-stakes testing on middle school mission and practice. *Research in Middle-Level Education Online, 34*(3), 1–10.

National Center for Education Statistics. (1993). *120 Years of American education: A statistical portrait.* Available at www.nces.ed.gov/pubsearch/pubsinfo.asp?pubid=93442

National Center for Education Statistics. (2011). *The nation's report card: Mathematics 2011* (NCES 2012–458). Washington, DC: National Center for Education Statistics, Institute of Education Sciences, U.S. Department of Education.

National Commission on Terrorist Attacks. (2004). *The 9/11 Commission report: Final report of the National Commission on Terrorist Attacks upon the United States.* New York, NY: W. W. Norton.

National Council of Teachers of Mathematics. (2000). *Principles and standards for school mathematics.* Reston, VA: Author.

National Education Technology Plan. (2010). *Transforming American education: Learning powered by technology.* Washington, DC: United States Department of Education.

National Governors Association Center for Best Practices, Council of Chief State School Officers. (2010). *Common Core State Standards.* Washington DC: Author.

National Park Service. (n.d.). Jim Crow. Available at www.nps.gov/malu/forteachers/jim_crow_laws.html

New London Group. (1996). A pedagogy of multiliteracies: Designing social futures. *Harvard Educational Review, 66*, 60–92.

Newkirk, T. (2010). The case for slow reading. *Educational Leadership, 67*(6), 6–11.

No Flying No Tights. (2013). Comics and manga vocabulary. Available at www.noflying-notights.com/comics-101/comics-manga-vocabulary-2/

Nokes, J. D. (2010). Preparing novice history teachers to meet students' literacy needs. *Reading Psychology, 31*, 493–523.

Nokes, J. D., Dole, J. A., & Hacker, D. J. (2007). Teaching high school students to use heuristics while reading historical texts. *Journal of Educational Psychology, 99*, 492–504.

Norris, S. P., & Phillips, L. M. (2003). How literacy in its fundamental sense is central to scientific literacy. *Science Education, 87,* 224–240.

O'Brien, D. (2001). "At-risk" adolescents: Redefining competence through the multiliteracies of intermediality, visual arts, and representation. *Reading Online, 4*(11). Available at www.readingonline.org/newliteracies/lit_Index.asp?HREF=/newliteracies/Obrien/index.html

Olson, J. C. (2008). *The comic strip as a medium for promoting science literacy.* Available at www.csun.edu/~jco69120/coursework/697/projects/OlsonActionResearchFinal.pdf

Özdemir, E. (2010). The effect of instructional comics on sixth grade students' achievement in heat transfer. Doctoral dissertation, Middle East Technical University. Available at etd.lib.metu.edu.tr/upload/12611749/index.pdf

Pearson, P. D., Moje, E., & Greenleaf, C. (2010, April). Literacy and science: Each in the service of the other. *Science, 328,* 459–463.

Pearson Prentice Hall. (2007). *Prentice Hall literature: The American experience.* Upper Saddle River, NJ: Author.

Pellegrino, J. W. (2006). Rethinking and redesigning curriculum, instruction and assessment: What contemporary research and theory suggests. Available at www.skillscommission.org/pdf/commissioned_papers/Rethinking%20and%20Redesigning.pdf

Pelton, L. F., & Pelton, T. (2009). The learner as teacher: Using student authored comics to "teach" mathematics concepts. In G. Siemens & C. Fulford (Eds.), *Proceedings of world conference on educational multimedia, hypermedia and telecommunications 2009* (pp. 1591–1599). Chesapeake, VA: Association for the Advancement of Computing in Education. Available at www.editlib.org/p/31690

Pelton, T., & Francis Pelton, L. (2006). Product review: Comic life deluxe. *Leading and Learning with Technology, 34*(1), 40–41.

Peterson, S. E., & Miller, J. A. (2004). Comparing the quality of students' experiences during cooperative learning and large-group instruction. *The Journal of Educational Research, 97*(3), 123–133.

Pilgreen, J. (2000). *The SSR handbook: How to organize and manage a sustained silent reading program.* Portsmouth, NH: Heinemann.

Pilgrim, D. (2012). *Who was Jim Crow?* Available at www.ferris.edu/news/jimcrow/who.htm

Prensky, M. (2005–2006). Listen to the natives. *Educational Leadership, 63*(4), 8–13.

Purves, A. C. (1998). *The web of text and the web of God: An essay on the third information transformation.* New York, NY: Guilford Press.

Reading Quest. (2013). Strategies for reading comprehension: Think-Pair-Share. Available at www.readingquest.org/strat/tps.html

Reid, C., & Macdonald, H. (2010). C2E2 debut draws 27,500: 2009 graphic novel sales down. *Publishers Weekly.* Available at www.publishersweekly.com/pw/by-topic/industry-news/comics/article/42894-c2e2-debuts-draws-27-500-2009-graphic-novel-sales-down.html

Reveles, J. M., Cordova, R., & Kelly, G. J. (2004). Science literacy and academic identity formulation. *Journal of Research in Science Teaching, 41,* 1111–1144.

Rosen, E. (2009). The narrative intersection of image and text: Teaching panel frames in comics. In S. E. Tabachnick (Ed.), *Teaching the graphic novel* (pp. 58–66). New York, NY: Modern Language Association.

Rosenfeld, J. A., & Mason, C. E. (2013, April 7). Who owns your DNA? Not who you think. *The Washington Post*, p. A21.

Rothman, R. (2012). Laying a common foundation for success. *Phi Delta Kappan, 94*(3), 57–61.

Rowe, R. C. (2005). A soft approach to hard science? *Drug Discovery Today, 10*, 309–311.

Rumelhart, D. E. (1978). *Schemata: The building blocks of cognition.* San Diego, CA: University of California, Center for Human Information Processing.

Scholastic. (2013). Using graphic novels with children and teens: A resource for teachers and librarians. Available at www.scholastic.com/teachers/lesson-plan/using -graphic-novels-children-and-teens-guide-teachers-and-librarians

Scholz, C. (1985, November 10). Comic books: Philosophy in a small balloon [Review of the book *Maus: A survivor's tale*]. *The Washington Post*, p. BW18.

Schultz, K. (2002). Looking across space and time: Reconceptualizing literacy learning in and out of school. *Research in the Teaching of English, 36*, 356–390.

Schwarz, G. E. (2002). Graphic novels for multiple literacies. *Journal of Adolescent and Adult Literacy, 46*, 262–265.

Sengul, S. (2011). Effects of concept cartoons on mathematics self-efficacy of 7th grade students. *Educational Sciences: Theory and Practice, 11*, 2305–2313.

Serafini, F., & Giorgis, C. (2003). *13 good reasons to read aloud with older readers.* Portsmouth, NH: Heinemann.

Seyfried, J. (2008). Reinventing the book club: Graphic novels as educational heavy-weights. *Knowledge Quest, 36*(3), 44–48.

Shanahan, T., & Shanahan, C. (2008). Teaching disciplinary literacy to adolescents: Rethinking content area literacy. *Harvard Education Review, 78*, 40–59.

Shanahan, T., & Shanahan, C. (2012). What is disciplinary literacy and why does it matter? *Topics in Language Disorders, 32*(1), 7–18.

Siegel, M., & Fonzi, J. (1995). The practice of reading in an inquiry-oriented mathematics class. *Reading Research Quarterly, 30*, 632–673.

Simmons, T. (2003). Comic books in my library? *PNLA Quarterly, 67*(12), 20.

Sipe, R. B. (2009). *Adolescent literacy at risk: The impact of standards.* Urbana, IL: National Council of Teachers of English.

Smith, M. S., Bill, V., & Hughes, E. K. (2008). Thinking through a lesson: Successfully implementing high-level tasks. *Mathematics Teaching in the Middle School, 14*(3), 132–138.

Song, Y., Heo, M., Krumenaker, L., & Tippins, D. (2008). Cartoons—an alternative learning assessment. *Science Scope, 32*(1), 16–21.

Strickland, D., & Alvermann, D. E. (Eds.). (2004). *Bridging the literacy achievement gap, grades 4–12.* New York, NY: Teachers College Press.

Thompson, T. (2008). *Adventures in graphica: Using comics and graphic novels to teach comprehension, 2–6.* Portland, ME: Stenhouse.

Toh, T. L. (2009). Use of cartoons and comics to teach algebra in mathematics classrooms. Available at www.mav.vic.edu.au/files/conferences/2009/12Toh.pdf

Vacca, R., & Vacca, J. (1999). *Content area reading.* New York, NY: Longman.

VanSledright, B. A., & Kelly, C. (1998). Reading American history: The influence of multiple sources on six fifth graders. *The Elementary School Journal, 98*(3), 239–265.

Vasudevan, L., & Campano, G. (2009). The social production of adolescent risk and the promise of adolescent literacies. *Review of Research in Education, 33*(1), 310–353.

Vygotsky, L. S. (1962). *Thought and language.* Cambridge MA: MIT Press.

Vygotsky, L. S. (1978). *Mind in society: The development of higher psychological processes.* Cambridge, MA: Harvard University Press.

Walker, N., & Bean, T. W. (2002, December). Sociocultural influences in content area teachers' selection and use of multiple texts. Paper presented at the 52nd annual National Reading Conference, Miami, FL.

Webb, P. (2009). Towards an integrated learning strategies approach to promoting scientific literacy in the South African context. *International Journal of Environmental and Science Education, 4*(3), 313–334.

Wertham, F. (1954). *Seduction of the innocent.* New York, NY: Rinehart.

Wineburg, S. (1998). Reading Abraham Lincoln: An expert/expert study in the interpretation of historical texts. *Cognitive Science, 22*(3), 319–346.

Wineburg, S. (2001). *Historical thinking and other unnatural acts: Charting the future of teaching the past.* Philadelphia, PA: Temple University Press.

Wineburg, S. (1991). On the reading of historical texts: Notes on the breach between school and academy. *American Educational Research Journal, 28,* 495–519.

Witkowski, J. A. (1997). Deconstructing the flowing line: Cartoons in biochemistry. *Trends in Biochemical Science, 22*(1), 142–146.

Worthy, J., & Prater, K. (2002). "I thought about it all night": Readers theatre for reading fluency and motivation. *The Reading Teacher, 56,* 294–297.

Wright, B. (2001). *Comic book nation.* Baltimore, MD: Johns Hopkins Press.

Yang, G. (2008). Graphic novels in the classroom. *Language Arts, 85,* 185–192.

Yoon, J-C. (2002). Three decades of sustained silent reading: A meta-analytic review of the effects of SSR on attitude toward reading. *Reading Improvement, 39*(4), 186–195.

Yore, L. D., & Treagust, D. F. (2006). Current realities and future possibilities: Language and science literacy—empowering research and informing instruction. *International Journal of Science Education, 28,* 291–314.

Zenkov, K., Bell, A., Harmon, J., Ewaida, M., & Fell, M. (2011). Seeing our city students and school: Using photography to engage diverse youth with our English classes. *English Education, 43,* 369–389.

Zickuhr, K., Rainie, L., Purcell, K., Madden, M., & Brenner, J. (2012). *Younger Americans' reading and library habits.* Available at www.libraries.pewinternet.org/2012/10/23/younger-americans-reading-and-library-habits/

Index

About the Authors

William G. Brozo is a professor of literacy in the Graduate School of Education at George Mason University in Fairfax, Virginia. He has taught reading and language arts in the Carolinas. He is the author of numerous articles and books on literacy development for children and young adults, including *To Be a Boy, to Be a Reader*. His newest book is *RTI and the Adolescent Reader: Responsive Literacy Instruction in Secondary Schools*. Dr. Brozo's research focuses on adolescent literacy, content area/disciplinary literacy, and the literate lives of boys.

Gary Moorman is currently professor emeritus at Appalachian State University in Boone, North Carolina. He retired in June 2012, after 32 years at the university. His publications appear in many professional journals, including *Reading Research Quarterly, Reading Research and Instruction, Journal of Reading, Reading Teacher, Reading Psychology,* and *Review of Research in Education*. He has written three books and edited a fourth. He served as the Online Communities Director for *Reading Online*, the International Reading Association's online journal, and as an editor of the *Yearbook of the American Reading Forum*. He has served on the editorial review boards for *Journal of Adolescent and Adult Literacy, ReadWriteThink, Journal of Educational Research, Reading Research and Instruction, Reading Psychology,* and *Teaching and Teacher Education*. He is interested and involved in international education efforts, participating in projects in Poland, Macedonia, Qatar, Egypt, and Bolivia.

Carla K. Meyer is an assistant professor at Appalachian State University in the Reading Education and Special Education Department. Her research appears in many professional journals, including *Journal of Adolescent and Adult Literacy* and *Action in Teacher Education*. She has coauthored three book chapters. She serves on the review board for *Journal of Adolescent and Adult Literacy, Literacy Research Association Yearbook,* and *Reading in the Middle*. She is currently co-chair of American Reading Forum's annual conference. Her research interests include content area literacy, young adult literature, and the intersection of educational policy and adolescent literacy.